THE CRISIS OF REFORMATION

The Crisis of Reformation: Confrontation and Conciliation

George D. Balsama
Jerome Friedman

Kent State University

KENDALL/HUNT PUBLISHING COMPANY
DUBUQUE, IOWA

To
Buffy
and
Fannie Sue

Contents

Preface

The concepts of toleration, compromise, and conciliation could generate little enthusiasm or sympathy on
the part of most Reformation and Counter-Reformation
figures. The sixteenth century was clearly the era of the
highly inspired and even fanatical: Luther, Carlstadt,
Zwingli, Calvin, Beza, Knox, Béda, Caraffa, ...
In opposition or at least contradistinction to these
religious crusaders arose a progression of more malleable
individuals: scholars, humanists, concerned intellectuals
of many types, sadly witnessing the plight of the Church
Universal. These men heroically strove to eliminate its
manifold deficiencies through the submission of reme-
dial suggestions, amounting to an ecclesiastical blueprint
for basically nondestructive, evolutionary change. However, although the positions set forth by such moderates
were as legitimate and intellectually valid as those of the
founding fathers of Reformation Protestantism, the
former were all but ignored; their proponents, scorned
and abused.

As the winds of religious self-righteousness and intolerance intensified, their bitter legacy rapidly became
poignantly evident in the political affairs of major European states. The impact was devastating. Its long term
effects, if not checked, could only lead the states into
the bloodiest anarchy.

By this time intellectuals and religious figures had already demonstrated their virtual inability to come to terms with the Pandora's box that their more rambunctious fellow travelers had ripped open. It became progressively more apparent that the problems, created by unbridled religious exuberance, would ultimately be resolvable only through the efforts of hard-headed, pragmatic realists, functioning within a basically nonreligious, nonideological framework. Even then, the battle that had to be fought in order to impose varieties of compromise upon inspired, militant, and at times obscenely opportunistic Europeans required herculean efforts, supplemented by large doses of fortitude.

* * * * *

The purpose of this book is to present to the introductory student certain key aspects of the Reformation era in light of the observations that have been made above. Specifically, its main thrust will hopefully demonstrate that by prevailing in its struggle against the forces for moderation, intellectual fanaticism helped convert and mutate a purely religious controversy into one which, in order to be settled, demanded the talents of such consummate practitioners of secular politics as Catherine de Medici, Elizabeth I of England, and Henry IV of France. Their reactions to the crises that beset the states over which they presided will be exposited, scrutinized, and evaluated.

* * * * *

The authors would like to express their gratitude to Professors Barrett Beer and Samuel Osgood, both of Kent State University, who kindly read portions of the manuscript and rendered them invaluable advice. They also wish to thank Professor David Greenstein of Roger Williams College, who gave so willingly of his time to edit several chapters. They are happy to acknowledge their debt to Miss Sue Helder, an exemplary student who helped them indefatigably with countless important details. To their wives, who dauntlessly poured over their illegible scrawl and performed the arduous service of typing, a very special note of thanks must be recorded. Finally, formal recognition cannot convey the extent to which two diffident authors are indebted to their mentors, Professor William F. Church of Brown University and Professor Robert M. Kingdon of The University of Wisconsin, whose insights, inspiration, and patience will not soon be forgotten.

George D. Balsama

Jerome Friedman

Kent State University

Introduction:

THE ROOTS OF THE CRISIS

Considering the importance of the Catholic Church throughout the Middle Ages and the amazing resources it had at its disposal, it is difficult to fathom how this institution fell upon such bad times in the early sixteenth century. Yet on the other hand, the success of the German Protestant Reformation does not seem incomprehensible. How then did the Catholic Church decline from its greatness of the thirteenth century to a position of such vulnerability that in 1517 an obscure Augustinian monk was able to turn it and much of Europe upside down? Contemporaries often pointed to its many abuses and signs of decay with which the Church either could not, or simply refused to, deal. Its weaknesses, however, in reality cut far deeper.

The transformation of the Church from a vital, resilient institution into an empty corrupted shell took about two hundred years, during which those entrusted with its guidance made virtually every mistake and miscalculation possible. In part then the despicable condition of the Renaissance Church resulted from lackluster leadership. Indeed by the early fourteenth century it was woefully evident that those men elected to the Papacy were simply not of the same caliber as in earlier days. Because the problems they faced were extremely serious, poor quality fourteenth century popes led the Church through a series of disasters.

The first cataclysm came in 1296 when King Philip the Fair of France attempted to tax the French clergy. The purpose of this new policy was two-fold. First, Philip hoped to bolster the royal treasury. Medieval monarchs were often quite impoverished since, as feudal lords in a decentralized manorial economy, they could tax nothing more than their own domains, which in Philip's case amounted to only a meager strip of land in central France. Second, the French Monarch desperately wanted to consolidate his position and authority. Plagued by powerful feudal nobles, he and his predecessors often found themselves at a disadvantage both economically and militarily. However, by commanding the personnel and resources of the very rich Church Philip hoped to strengthen his own position vis à vis his arrogant vassals.

The clergy reacted predictably and refused to cooperate with the King. An ensuing conflict soon became so ferocious that in time the Papacy itself felt obliged to intervene, warning Philip to alter his policies. When the King refused, His Holiness issued in November 1302 the famous bull *Unum Sanctum*, which excommunicated him. Philip however reacted by ignoring papal sentiments and ordering his agents to kidnap the Pope, the shock of which brought about the latter's death within a month. The next pope was strictly a short-term pontiff, dying probably as a result of poison a few months after his election. In the ensuing interregnum, the wily French King succeeded in forcing the election of a French pope, who took the name Clement V (1305-14) and set up a new papal capital at Avignon, in southern France.

The Church, of course, suffered greatly from this experience. Not only was this proud institution humiliated by its obvious subservience to and dependence upon France, it now faced numerous other problems with which it had not previously had to contend. In the past, money to meet its operating expenses had been supplied by Roman bankers at reasonable rates of interest. However, with the Church now located in Avignon, credit from Roman bankers was generally not forthcoming. As a result the Church found it necessary to borrow at very high rates of interest, which could only be paid back by greatly increasing existing taxes and by creating many new ones. Moreover, since Church revenues were used to build a new, magnificent papal court, the increase in taxation was not well received anywhere in Christendom.

The Avignonese Papacy also became an unwilling anvil in international relations. At this time England and France were locked in the seemingly endless Hundred Years War. Understandably suspicious of both the French Pope and his new taxes, the English hesitated to send gold into the realm of their enemy.

In 1377, under great international pressure, the curia travelled to Rome to elect a new pope. As the court convened, Roman mobs beseiged its meeting place demanding selection of an Italian. Out of fear for their lives even the French cardinals chose Urban VI, an Italian, to be pope. Immediately after the election however the curia returned to France, where it nullified the election for the obvious reasons and promptly chose a new pontiff, this time a Frenchman taking the name, Clement VII. Unfortunately, Urban VI continued to enjoy Italian support and would not abdicate his position. Instead he re-established the "Church of Rome," while the "Church of Avignon" was still in existence. This plurality of popes, known by historians as the Great Schism, divided the Christian world into two camps. Half of Europe was loyal to Clement, while the other half followed Urban's leadership. Each pope excoriated and excommunicated the other, and attempted to collect taxes from all Europeans.

This deplorable situation continued until 1409, when

conditions actually took a turn for the worse. In this year an ecumenical council was called to meet in Pisa for the purpose of deposing the two existing popes and electing a new one. The council carried out its charge and a new pope, Alexander V, was elected. Regrettably, both other popes refused to abdicate, leaving the Church with three heads. Even worse, Alexander died abruptly, and in his place the council chose John XXIII, all of which dashed any attempt to end the Great Schism, for it was soon discovered that John had spent his earlier years as a pirate.

Five years later a new council was called to meet in Constance in order to depose John XXIII, the French pope, and the Italian pope. In place of the three pretenders the new council installed Martin V. Both John and the other Italian pope abdicated; and although the French pope refused, he immediately lost the support of the King of France, which all but isolated him. A few years later he died in Spain. At long last there was one pope over one Catholic Church.

Yet, though the organizational and institutional divisions were healed, the basic problems facing the Church continued to grow. The prestige of the pontificate had during the past decades so badly deteriorated that even local religious leadership was questioned. The new taxes, the recriminations, the mass excommunications, all deeply planted seeds of doubt in the minds of many. Well founded reports that the revenues raised through new taxation were being used to support the gambling habits and prostitutes of many cardinals and bishops in Avignon and Rome did little to soothe the questioning consciences of troubled laymen.

This general aura of doubt was partially expressed through the phenomenal growth of anticlericalism and heresy. John Wycliffe in England preached governmental control over many Church activities and ecclesiastical wealth. Needless to say, rich nobles as well as the monarchy favored any plan which would deliver Church lands and wealth into their own hands, especially if it also was for the greater glory of God. Wycliffe's followers, the Lollards, developed as a substitute for official Catholicism, a very down to earth approach to religion, fortified with a heretical English translation of the Bible and the service of lay preachers.

Anticlerical sentiment spread from one country to another, and soon what were in the past very "healthy" regions like Bohemia, became hotbeds of heresy. In this country John Huss taught a religious belief similar to that of Wycliffe and rapidly succeeded removing his many followers from the Catholic fold.

There were many Churchmen who believed that since the ecumenical council had proved so successful an institution for dealing with the plurality of popes, it might be equally effective in curtailing the growth of abuse-induced heresy. At the Council of Constance these conciliarists passed several laws limiting the powers of the Papacy so that the Church might never be exploited again as it had been by Philip. The decree of *Sacrosancta* (1415) made the ecumenical council the highest and most authoritative institution within the Church, ostensibly assigning the Papacy a subservient position. The decree of *Frequens* (1417) established the council as a permanent part of Church government, which had to be called into session by the pope on a regular basis. These decrees generated a great feeling of optimism in many circles within the Church hierarchy, for it was believed that permanent councils would revolutionize religious life. No pope could be too corrupt, and no abuses could grow too gross, without being attended to by a council committee. Some even spoke of a new era of representative Church government to replace current papal autocracy.

This optimism was short-lived. In accordance with the decrees of Constance Martin called a council in 1423 to meet in Pavia. Unhappy about his less exalted position, Martin did everything he could to weaken the council, and soon after the bishops had assembled in Pavia His Holiness moved the council to Sienna. Many bishops were too old to make the trip while others were forced to return to their diocese thus making Sienna a most under-represented council. This gave Martin a good excuse to dissolve this ecumenical meeting before it could further deteriorate his position.

Again in 1431 Martin called a council to meet in Basle, in accordance with the decree of *Frequens*. The Pope died during its meetings, but his successor, Eugenius IV, attempted a Martin-like ploy by moving the council to Bologna in 1433. Many prelates were stunned, for it was incomprehensible that the Pope would play politics when central Europe was turning to heresy. A number of bishops refused to move to Bologna and continued holding sessions in Basle, where even Hussite representatives were invited to analyze their differences with Catholic orthodoxy. These discussions went so well that a compromise solution was reached, which was acceptable to large numbers of Bohemians. In a mood of great confidence, the ecclesiastics at Basle invited the leadership of the Greek Orthodox Church to join them for discussions, which also met with a great measure of success.

All these accomplishments irritated the Pope, who feared the important successes of the recalcitrant and rebellious bishops meeting in Basle. In attempting to stave off any future triumphs, Eugenius dissolved the council. The reaction at Basle was negative, the bishops countering by limiting the pope's power of taxation, and electing another pope, Felix V. It seemed to many that the Church was once again divided with a plurality of pontificates.

Fortunately for the Church this new power struggle resolved itself. The representatives meeting at Basle could not remain there indefinitely; and in time their opposition, and conciliarism, in general, melted away, leaving the pope in a position of supremacy. Some Catholic historians have argued that the consolidation of power in the hands of a single supreme pope was essential before reform could be carried out. This view loses much credibility when one scrutinizes the nature of the strengthened pontificate, and its nonexistent desires for self-improvement. No councils were called for the purpose of reform, nor were any commissions appointed to study the problems besetting the Church. Similarly, not one pope struck out against the ubiquitous corruption, now that it was in his power to do so. It was not until 1512 that the next ecumenical council was called, by Julius II; but this dealt only with local administrative problems, though it remained in session until the time of the Reformation five years later. There was no attempt to solve any of the problems of abused power or authority, nor was there any awareness that such activity should be forthcoming. When Pope Leo X was presented with Luther's call for reform in 1517, the pontiff lethargically answered that he was not interested in monks' squabbles.

Though it may seem incredible that Church leadership was unaware of the depth of anticlericalism and heresy, there is one possible explanation for this state of affairs. When the Papacy returned from Avignon, the new Italian leadership resolved never to permit a similar situation to occur again. Rather than electing saintly and religious men to the pontificate, the curia chose capable administrators and financial wizards. It was hoped that a succession of such individuals might put the new Church on a sound financial footing and in a solid international position. Though this choice of direction is understandable, it almost inevitably led to disastrous results. The renewed economic and political strength of Rome came at the cost of religious sensibility and sensitivity. The Church became saturated with so many fiscal and moral abuses that soon a decadent religious condition became the norm.

Three popes in particular have been cited by historians as representative of this new Renaissance Papacy and as particularly immoral. Alexander VI of the bloody Borgia family was pope from 1492 to 1503, and lived such a scandalous life that he himself boasted he would go to hell. Since he mistrusted everyone, he gave the important position of Regent of the Papal States to his favorite illegitimate son, Pedro. He also provided his other bastards with attractive sinecures.

Julius II followed Alexander. Scion of the famous della Rovera family, he served as pope from 1503 to 1513, and succeeded in commissioning the talented Michelangelo. When not admiring the art of his craftsmen he often donned his suit of armor and led his papal army in its maneuvers or battles. Not a single-minded man, Julius too fathered many bastards.

Following Julius, Leo X became pope from 1513 to 1521 and had the good fortune to preside over the Catholic Church during Luther's rebellion. He was of the important Florentine banking family, the Medicis; and like Julius was an art patron, responsible for popularizing Raphael. Unlike his immediate predecessor, the Medici Pope was more interested in hunting than fighting, so he ordered his private apartment adorned with murals of hunting scenes. He too managed to fill much of his time with gambling and whoring.

It should be understood that these three gentlemen were not particularly immoral by the standards of their times. Their vices were generally representative of aristocratic life in the Renaissance, and all three were typical of their class. Cortese for instance, in writing a guide book for future cardinals, mentions that a serious candidate for that holy office should have at least one hundred forty servants to cater to his needs, and an income of at least twelve thousand ducats a year to sustain gambling loses.

In a short time the Church hierarchy was filled with bankers, diplomats, and political opportunists. By 1500 the bent of the Church personnel seemed to contemporaries to be turned towards making money and building a position in a powerful Church organization. With such leadership, abused authority, bribery, and fiscal irregularity became a way of life, as the Church itself was converted into a commodity to be bought and sold. Simony, the selling of Church offices, was so common that it was rumored anyone wishing to purchase a bishopric had only to consult the *Papal Colletoria* to determine the going rate for such a position and what revenues it might bring in. Similarly, nepotism was rampant because many Church officials felt they could only trust their cousins or other relatives in important positions. Just as some wealthy persons bought bishoprics for their ten year old sons as an investment, others appointed their four year old nephews to important positions in order to consolidate their own power. The results of this high level abuse were soon evident in the local parish. Bishop absenteeism was very common, as might be expected of a ten year old or a business man. Similarly, there was a great deal of pluralism, for many found two or ten bishoprics even more profitable than one.

There were still other ways to increase profits in the typical diocese: local Church taxes might be increased; services could be cut back; and the prices of those remaining could be raised. Most often clerical seminaries were closed, or reduced in size, with the result that priestly illiteracy became a fairly general phenomenon. Often a local priest knew the Mass and several other services by heart but was otherwise totally ignorant about the Catholic religion.

Equally depressing was the lack of priests. In some parts of France and northern Germany there was one

priest for every dozen parishes, and there were cases of
fifty parishes sharing the services of a single cleric. As a
result many were baptized at a late age, had to wait
months or years to get married, and died without the
last rites. And when a priest did come to a small village
many parishioners found they could not afford to have
him perform necessary rituals. It is therefore not at all
surprising that there was widespread resentment against
the Church, and a general feeling that Rome was out of
touch with the needs of the people.

This was the situation on the eve of the Reformation.
Fortunately, these abuses did not go unnoticed by all
members of the Church hierarchy; and there were occa-
sional calls for reform. The important question in 1500
was whether reform would come from within the
Church, or whether revolution would be needed to bring
about the changes that it so desperately needed.

I

THE BEGINNING OF THE CRISIS:
FIRST STIRRINGS, FIRST DIVISION

In 1537 the Spanish Inquisition forbade the reading of Erasmus' works in Spanish and expurgated his Latin writings. Twenty-two years later Pope Paul IV prohibited Catholics from reading all Erasmian treatises, even those unrelated to religion; and the Council of Trent, called to combat the growth of Lutheranism, reacted similarly by placing Erasmus' religious opus on the Index of Prohibited Books in the very same year. St. Ignatius Loyola himself, the leading personality of the Catholic reform movement, related the manner in which he "nearly froze" upon reading Erasmus' works because of their lack of true devotion.

Although it is strange that a man who consistently maintained his fidelity to Catholicism was able to evoke such violent Catholic sentiment against himself, an examination of his writings and views can clarify this peculiar situation. Erasmus wrote satire and irony, and those he attacked did not appreciate his fine wit— especially when his comments were accurate. Nowhere is his biting pen more evident than in his essay of 1514, *In Praise of Folly*, where Erasmus portrayed society from the vantage point of foolishness by taking the reader on a personal tour through many social institutions and pointing out how ridiculous the antics of different professions must seem to the outsider.

There is virtually no class or profession that is not exposed to derision and laughter.

When writing about theologians Erasmus expressed the thoughts of many people in chiding the former for shaping and reshaping scripture to whatever view they held at the moment. He condemned their hair-splitting logic chopping, and questioned their ability to discuss so profoundly things they knew nothing about. As an example he cited how theologians dealt with hell: "They draw exact pictures of every part of hell, as though they had spent many years in that region. They also create new heavenly regions as imagination dictates . . . there must be a place for the blessed souls to take walks, to entertain at dinner, or even play a game of ball."

Erasmus criticized theologians from extensive first-hand experience, for he had spent many years at the University of Paris studying for a doctorate in theology and was amazed at how trivial and irrelevant discussions could be. Could God have become incarnated in a stone or a cucumber rather than in a man? What will be the exact date and hour of the final judgment? How did God know what to create? Erasmus found such themes absurd and the method of argument repugnant. That these men should be taken seriously seemed unbelievable to him.

Erasmus satirized monks as well, and again was able to speak from firsthand experience. The term "religious" was inappropriate for monks, he said, "since for the most part they stay as far away from religion as possible." The monk was so detested "that accidentally meeting one is considered to be bad luck, though the monks themselves believe that they are magnificent creatures." Monks are described as forever congratulating themselves on their "Christian poverty" but are always found sponging off everyone else while they get drunk and live immorally. The sum total of their religious life is nothing but a pretense where "the members of one order will denounce the members of another order clamorously because of the way in which the habit [robe] has been belted or the slightly darker color of it."

Erasmus reprehended theologians and monks, but these were not the only corrupted members of the Church leadership. Indeed, they were corrupt because their superiors were even more so than they; therefore, Erasmus was no kinder in his treatment of bishops. "If our bishops would but stop and consider what their white albs signify, namely sincerity and the pure life . . . they would not lead such troubled and shameful lives. But as it is they are kept too busy feeding themselves to think of these things." The author was the first to admit, however, that bishops did not spend *all* their time thinking of feeding their stomachs; they also kept a close watch on their money. "When it comes to financial matters they truly act the part of the bishop to the hilt, overseeing everything—and overlooking nothing."

Erasmus also denounced those bishops who had been made cardinals and is full of wonder that the Pope always managed to choose the very worst of the lot, but this too was no coincidence. "The Popes of our time still insist on profanely attaching the name Peter [the apostle] to territories, cities, wages, and all other money. These are the things they fight to uphold with fire, sword, and blood—inflamed by a zeal for Christ, of course— . . . bragging that they have routed the enemies of the Church, as if the Church had any greater enemies than these charlatan Popes." These were strong words; and though others had been critical of the Pope's disproportionate interest in money and land, none dared call the Pope the true enemy of the Church and a charlatan. If the Pope was corrupt it followed that other Church officials would emulate His Holiness, realizing that they would not be reproached. Therefore, just as the Popes went off to war to gain land and money in the

name of Christ, "the priests feel it is sacrilegious to be in
a lesser state of holiness than their prelates, so they too
go off to war in the best military manner." Priests, like
Popes, were also ingenious in their ability to convince
everyone how much money was due them, all in the
name of Christ of course.

However caustic his attacks on those church officials
who seemed more interested in gold than God, Erasmus
was no emeny of the Catholic religion but a deeply
conscientious man moved to criticize the Church because he felt it should and could be better than it was.
As he saw it, the basic problem was that the Catholic
Church was too tied to external rituals, refusing to em-
phasize sufficiently the inward spirit. These external
rituals had to be performed in order for the believer to
gain entry into heaven, so the priests charged money for
their services thus converting the Church into a profitable business. Erasmus may or may not have been justified in claiming the Church's interest was only super-
ficial and not spiritual, but certainly this was a very
widely held view in the sixteenth century.

For over a thousand years Christianity had been interpreted by the Catholic Church to be an institutional
religion, which is to say that aside from the need for
personal belief and commitment, a good Christian had
to receive the services of the Church for salvation. Since
man was tainted by the effects of original sin and therefore deficient in his ability to do good on his own,
righteousness had to come from outside man, from the
Church via a priest. If a person was baptised a Catholic
by a priest, God's grace, or divine aid, was transmitted
to the individual. Similarly, a person wishing forgiveness
for some evil act committed might feel contrite, but
could only be absolved by confessing to a priest and
doing penance. Even a righteous person, wishing to lead
a life along more Christian lines by receiving God's help
through Communion, could only receive this aid by at-

tending the Church to be present at Mass. Lastly, when a Christian dies he must receive last rites from a priest. The latter is so central to the religious life of any Catholic desiring salvation that the Church has set him apart in a separate class or caste of those divinely ordained individuals who have contact with God. Unfortunately, this also institutionalizes and freezes the gap between the average Christian and God, making the intervention of the priest necessary. Without the priest and the rituals he performs for the lay Christian no salvation is possible.

How did the priest receive so much authority and importance? According to Catholic belief Christ built the Church in this world on Peter, who was the founder of the Church of Rome. God granted to Peter and to his successors great divine power "to loosen or to bind" as they saw fit. The Pope shared much of this power with all other bishops who in turn annointed priests and in this way provided the layman with a direct link between his priest and God, as well as assured man's dependency upon the priest. It is obvious that such great reliance can lead to abuses. Throughout the Middle Ages priests had charged for their services, and during the fifteenth and sixteenth centuries this practice became, in many cases, actual exploitation. Since at this time the financial situation of the Church was desperate, the Papacy increasingly taxed local churches, the result being that regular services of the priest increased in cost. The lay Christian was forced to pay, for without the sacraments he was in a state of sin—a condition he took very seriously and would try to avoid at any cost.

The Church exploited its unique position between God and man in other ways. In the Reformation period one could purchase an indulgence, or a remission of the time one would have to spend being punished in the next world. In the past these indulgences were granted sparingly, only to those who had performed an extraor-

dinary religious act, such as going on a crusade; but later
they were sold to anyone who could pay. By the sixteenth century there were salesmen all over Europe
hawking indulgences the way tradesmen sold leather
goods and livestock. One such salesman, John Tetzel,
even had a song to demonstrate the extraordinary effect
of indulgences:

> As soon as gold in the basin rings,
> Right then the soul to heaven springs.

The sale of indulgences grew so widespread that it became one of the factors that caused Martin Luther to
break with the Church. Many who bought these remissions felt there was no need to live religious lives since
"all was forgiven" and so very painlessly too. There
were even alleged cases of persons buying indulgences
for sins not yet committed, but anticipated!

Clearly then, Erasmus had some justification for feeling the Church had lost sight of its proper function—the
care of man's spirit and soul—and was instead becoming
involved with external rituals for monetary gain. But if
Erasmus was critical of all these practices yet claimed he
was a religious Christian, what did he believe? How
would he correct the current situation? To understand
his views and beliefs one should first briefly examine his
youth and educational background.

Erasmus' life did not have an auspicious beginning.
Born in Gouda, Holland in 1466, he was the illegitimate
son of a priest and physician's daughter. However,
though orphaned at an early age, he did receive an excellent education first in Gouda and later at the Cathedral
School of St. Lebwin's in Deventer. This school was part
of a network of institutions associated with an organization called the Brethren of the Common Life, founded
in the fourteenth century by the Dutch mystic Gerhard
Groote. It had been his intention to teach a practical
and spiritual approach to religion as a reaction to the

cold, logical, and scholastic tendency popular in his day.
Groote felt that all the erudition and learning would
make no one a better Christian or a better human being;
for morality and inward piety, the goals of religion, had
to be felt and experienced, not learned by rote. This
pietistic approach is best summed up by the Brethren's
most famous member Thomas à Kempis, who wrote in
his little book *In Imitation of Christ*, in 1425: "Of what
advantage is it to dispute profoundly about the trinity if
by your lack of humility you are all the while displeas-
ing the trinity?" What difference did it really make if
you understood how God was both three and one; how
the Son is *generated* from the Father from whom the
Spirit then *proceeds*? God demands not intellectual
erudition, but an ethical and moral life coupled with a
true love of Him and His creatures. If asked how a man
should live his life, Thomas à Kempis would say: "In
imitation of Christ".

Though Erasmus was not as anti-intellectual as many
of the Brethren, he did share their contempt for useless
learning and accepted their criticism of external rituals
and practices in favor of internal and spiritual religious
feeling. "We kiss the shoes of saints and their dirty
handkerchiefs, and we leave their books, their most holy
and effective relics neglected." How foolish it seemed to
attach so much importance to supposedly authentic
relics, like a thorn from Christ's crown or a thumbnail
reputed to have belonged to some ancient martyr. Yet
many wealthy and well meaning people spent fortunes
collecting relics. One German prince was reported to
have had a collection of 17,000 relics, but did this make
him a better Christian? Similarly, what was the use of
saying Mass and receiving grace in the Eucharist if the
recipient was full of hate for his fellow man and had no
intention of reforming his life?

It is in this context that we must view Erasmus' condemnation of the Church, for he asked how Christlike

was a pope who went off to war leading an army for
material gain? How valuable was the obscure reasoning
of puffed up theologians when in the Sermon on the
Mount Christ clearly stated that man should live a simple and ethical life? Did Christ charge a fee for baptising
children as priests did? Moreover, how could any bishop
justify his hoarding of power and wealth when Christ
admonished His true followers to give up their worldly
possessions and cares? What Erasmus wanted to teach
was a philosophy of Christ, the true acceptance of
Christlike behavior, for only then would religion and the
Church have real meaning.

In expounding his philosophy of Christ Erasmus rejected any overly intellectual approach to God since
there was no possible way to understand Him anyway,
or many of the things attributed to Him. On the other
hand Christ left a clear record and explanation of how
man should live, through His sayings, the Sermon on the
Mount, and the example He set throughout His life. The
reform Erasmus visualized was at the most basic level of
human understanding and consideration, a reformation
in the spirit of man.

In 1503 Erasmus published the *Handbook of the Militant Christian*, in which he outlined how one could live
like Christ. It was a totally serious work, devoid of his
usual wit and humor but nonetheless one of the most
popular books of the sixteenth century, which by 1585
had been translated from Latin into English, Spanish,
German, Dutch, and Polish. The central theme throughout is that the Christian must be "free and spontaneous,
unconstrained by external law" and ritual. "I have en-
deavored", Erasmus wrote, "to recall theology that has
fallen into sophisticated squabbling back to its source
and original simplicity." More than anything else the
book was an attempt to make the Christian religion
meaningful in the daily life of the Christian. Being pious

and religious did not imply leading a sheltered, clois-
tered existence, but living a full, yet spiritualized life.

Erasmus warns his reader that being truly religious is
not the same as performing many rituals and observances, and he says it is "sublimely stupid" to equate the
two for no ritual can be of any value "unless accompanied by internal piety." "There are far too many who
count up how many times they attend Mass and rely
entirely upon this." Neither can religious observances,
whatever their value, take the place of truly humane actions, "take for example a case where your brother is in
dire need of your help and you go on mumbling your
prayers, pretending not to notice his predicament. God
will actually despise that kind of prayer."

If being pious means being humane towards others, it
also means understanding one's own fears and weaknesses as well as those of others; and Erasmus points out
how even Peter denied and rejected Christ because he
feared death. Similarly, it is not evil to love; for love like
fear, is a part of man created in Christ's image. The
author says that when a man loves his spouse, rather
than being ashamed of his feelings he should rejoice, for
"you love the Christ in her." The very essence of life
itself is holy and should not be rejected but made spiritual and meaningful.

Why should these views be so offensive to the Catholic Church that Erasmus' works were condemned and
prohibited? One reason is that nowhere in his works
does Erasmus assign any importance to priests, rituals,
or the institutions of the Church. Many saw Erasmus
leading Christianity away from the Church by making
the latter unnecessary for salvation or for the fulfillment
of a Christian life. It is also true that many of these
critics were opposed to any kind of reform that would
make the Church even the slightest bit different than it
was. Others pointed out that Erasmus did not recognize

the importance of original sin as a negative factor in
man's personality because he showed how man could
act in a Christlike fashion through his own efforts.
Erasmus listened to these criticisms but was not
moved by them. He had not attacked the basic importance of priests and sacraments. He had merely empha-
sized the need for inward spirit; and if making a religion
inwardly meaningful was dangerous and had to be rejected, then surely there was something wrong with that
religion!

Why did he stay in the Catholic Church if he was so
severely criticized? The answer was quite simple. While
he could have become a Lutheran, as many others were,
he felt that such a move made little sense unless the new
faith was significantly better than the old. Since true
religion was a question of the heart and soul, there were
bound to be pious and impious people in both churches.
So Erasmus remained a Catholic who spent his time
with what he felt was important in a practical sense, like
paraphrasing the psalms in easy language for those who
had difficulty understanding the Bible.

Though Erasmus' ideas and desires for reform were
well known long before Martin Luther condemned the
Church and started his own sect, it was Luther and not
Erasmus who was to spearhead the Reformation. Martin
Luther had spent much of his early life obsessed with
being a good Christian; and he was a monk, a priest, and
an official in the Augustinian order. Like Erasmus before him, Luther was very dissatisfied with the condition of the Church, and agreed that reform was needed.
Though he had the admiration and respect of all who
knew him, Luther was uncomfortable in his relationship
with God and felt unsure of the Church's ability to help
him draw closer to God. He was an ideal Christian by all
standards; yet he felt that God must surely hate him, for
how else could he account for his feelings of guilt?

Long before 1517, when Luther actually broke with

the Church, he had been developing an approach to the questions of grace and salvation very different from that taught by the Church of his day. Based on his personal experiences Luther contended that grace could not come from acts and rituals; for if it could, he would have felt saintly rather than guilty. His conclusion that grace must come directly from God alone and not from the Church seemed especially logical since God was all powerful and man, just an evil and unimportant being. How could man presume to pressure God into bestowing grace simply by performing certain rituals, for did not God know if such a person was really deserving or not? Surely man was showing a little too much confidence in believing he could require God to grant him grace purely on the strength of his own actions. For Luther, God transmits grace to those He loves and denies it to those whom He does not love; and what man does through rituals and observances is secondary because God knows even without them who is deserving and who is not.

Luther had been developing these non-ritualistic ideas as early as 1512, and he summed up this approach through the belief that man must live by faith alone, which is to say, man had to have faith and hope that he was a beloved of God and that he would therefore receive grace. Man could not live by acts or good works because they assured nothing if God Himself had not already decided to grant grace and salvation.

The Catholic Church was not against these ideas. Indeed, such thoughts had been presented by others before Luther, though never with the same degree of disregard for Church institutions and hierarchy. In the past this tendency had been developed to supplement Catholic sacramental theology, much as Erasmus had hoped his pietistic philosophy of Christ would add strength to existing Catholic thought. Luther, however, believed his system of beliefs should replace all Catholic thought, or at least, that the Church's theology should be altered drastically. The one issue which made clear to Luther that there was no hope of compromise with the Church was that of indulgences. When Luther first heard of this practice from his students, he was positive they were mistaken or that the Pope was being misrepresented by his salesmen. Surely the Pope would not presume to sell remissions of God ordained sins or in any way abrogate God's will. Undoubtedly, Luther thought, the Pope had meant that the Church could grant remissions of sins and penalties imposed by the Church itself, not those of God.

During the next few years the Catholic Church made it quite clear to Luther that he was wrong in his presumptions about the Pope, for the latter most certainly saw no limitations on the possibilities for absolution through indulgences. In debates with Church representatives such as John Eck, Luther was forced to concede that if he did not believe that the Pope was all powerful—for if he were he could absolve man of all sins—then the entire Church itself was limited in its effectiveness. Furthermore, Luther gradually proved willing to admit that if the Church as a whole could not speak for God, then even such traditionally important institutions as the ecumenical council might not have any true validity and could err. Though these points of belief were wrung out of Luther in debate with a very skillful opponent, none was inconsistent with the views he had been developing. Over the next few years these views would act as the basis for a new Lutheran Church.

These events of 1517-1521 made Luther a hero to all who felt, as he did, that the Church was not an all powerful institution and that only God could grant salvation. Many applauded his logical individualistic approach to religion which dispensed with institutions, officials, and many rituals that only separated man from God. At this time many assumed that Luther and

Erasmus were of one mind since both attacked current religious practice on the grounds that rituals were ineffective. Indeed, one popular saying of the day was that "Erasmus laid the egg that Luther hatched," with Luther himself conceding as much in 1519 when he wrote to Erasmus for the first time: "I speak to you so often and you with me, Erasmus, our ornament and our hope, and yet we do not know each other . . . Erasmus, amiable man, if you think fit, acknowledge also this little brother in Christ, who admires you and feels friendly disposed to you, and for the rest would deserve no better because of his ignorance than to lie unknown, buried in a corner." Moreover, it appears that Erasmus was also favorably impressed with the radical young German monk for he wrote to one of Luther's friends: "I hope that your endeavors and those of your party will be successful . . . All the best minds are rejoicing at Luther's boldness."

While many liberal minded men saw great possibilities in Luther's attack upon the institutions of the Church and in a renewed interest in the inner spirit of the Christian man, many began to have misgivings about the course that Luther's reformation was taking. All congratulated Luther for freeing the Christian from the shackles of observances and rituals; but some anxiously realized that this was not the only change Luther had brought about.

Many feared that nothing less than civil and class war was in the making, with religion becoming the convenient excuse for political action. From the very beginning some German princes had declared their support of Luther against Catholic forces. Luther himself in his famous *Address to the German Nobility* asked independent German princes to rise up, institute the new religion, and fight against both the Catholic Church and those rulers who supported it. While many princes backed Luther out of great loyalty to the new Protestant faith, many others joined the movement simply because it offered them an excellent opportunity to consolidate power within their realms by confiscating rich Church property and monastic lands. Still others saw the Reformation as the perfect justification for working against the interests of the Catholic Emperor Charles V, head of the loose federation of German states. Similarly, there were princes prepared to fight against Luther not out of excessive religious zeal but because it suited their interests to keep either the Catholic Church or Charles V as strong as possible. Such a civil war in the Holy Roman Empire could have disastrous effects for all Germany, and it would not be the only secular consequence of a possible religious reformation.

For hundreds of years the peasants and artisans of central Europe had been bitter about their declining position under a decaying feudal economy. From 1521 to 1524 more than 300,000 German peasants finally rebelled against their dreadful condition. Throughout the fourteenth century there had been sporadic rebellions all across Europe such as the Watt-Tyler rebellion in England and the rising of the Jacquerie in France. When Martin Luther spoke of the "liberty of the Christian man" and asked for the overthrow of the Catholic Church, the employer of countless peasants, many took this as an indication that the new religion was calling for the abolition of all social restraints like feudalism, not merely the Catholic Mass. These peasant supporters of Luther were surprised and dismayed when he called upon the princes to put down this class rebellion, and many Europeans were shocked at the language Luther used in requesting wholesale peasant murder. The German reformer claimed the peasants had misunderstood him and that he spoke only in religious terms; but had he not called on the independent princes to rebel against Charles V?

Aside from civil war and social rebellion, there was

yet another element of concern about the new Reformation, that of the consequences resulting from a total split in Christianity. In their first flush of enthusiasm Lutherans were in no mood to compromise with the old religion and incorporate their desire for reform within a church they thought totally corrupt. Similarly, Catholic authorities felt Luther had committed the very worst of crimes in breaking Church discipline and by turning the Church against itself, no matter how significant the religious issues. They too were in no mood to compromise with a man they viewed as an upstart, a rabblerouser, a heretic, and the cause of much civil unrest. Many in the Church counselled that Luther should simply be ignored because although the Papacy had been threatened before by such heretics, they had always been crushed in the end. The intransigence on both sides inevitably led to the creation of a new Lutheran Church with its own practices, rituals, and traditions. The feeling of alienation between the two religions grew so that neither saw the value or possibility of compromise; nor did either side feel that any solution was possible, short of the total destruction of the other church.

Had the Lutheran Reformation been confined to a very small area, there would have been little danger; but the printing press, Luther's charismatic personality, and the desire for change on the part of princes and peasants all contributed to making Lutheranism instantly popular throughout Germany and central Europe. Moreover, the Reformation seemed to be spreading to other parts of Europe as well. Luther's tracts were soon read in England, France, Spain, Italy, and Poland; and there was every reason to believe that these countries too would be torn by civil and social war. Many envisioned Luther's call to reform being accepted by all the malcontented of Europe for political, social, and economic reasons, and imagined that Christendom would soon be a mass graveyard.

While some were willing to take up the call to reform and follow wherever it led, and others were willing to label all change heresy, there was yet a third group which saw that no matter what the outcome of the religious conflict, Europe would be no better off than before. Though reform was necessary, Luther was providing the spark for much more; and while none would fault Luther his idealism and enthusiasm, was civil war and chaos any easier to live with than an exploiting church? Was hatred between Christians and the division of families a fair price to pay for eliminating a few abuses? Were rival interpretations of the Bible sufficient reason to fill graveyards and create many new ones? How could any of these things be important when it was only the inner spirit of man which really counted?

Erasmus originally greeted the Lutheran Reformation with applause, but by 1521 he too began to have doubts, for Luther's kind of reform might prove much too costly. The latter was undoubtedly sincere, but his views were being used by too many other forces in society for one to judge the new religion solely on the basis of Lutheran beliefs. At first Erasmus tried to rationalize Luther's apparent radicalism, and the even greater radicalism accompanying Lutheranism, as being an unfortunate and regrettable part of change: "If as appears from the wonderful success of Luther's cause God wills all this, and He has perhaps judged such a drastic surgeon as Luther necessary for the corruption of these times, then it is not my business to withstand him." However, a short while later he would write: "I fear for the unfortunate Luther," because it was now clear how the reformer was inadvertently the cause of Germany's social unrest and was being used by different interest groups.

Despite Erasmus' reservations, the public generally believed that he stood behind Luther and all that was happening. His friend Vives, wrote him from the Netherlands: " . . . that you are looked upon as a Lutheran here is certain." A certain Nicholas of Egmond probably summed up general feeling when he wrote about Erasmus: "As long as he refuses to write against Luther we take him to be a Lutheran."

Erasmus had never ceased hoping that Luther would somehow become reconciled with the Catholic Church and that the split in Christendom might be healed; but by the mid-1520's almost all prominent people had taken one side or the other. He attempted to maintain a middle position, hoping that his influence with both Catholics and Lutherans might facilitate some reconciliation; but each passing day made such hopes more unrealistic. Erasmus was also growing old and becoming tired of this conflict, which seemed to drain its participants, while he found himself under increasing pressure to side with one group or the other. Moreover, as Europe became more polarized, many grew irritated with Erasmus' refusal to join the battle. A friend warned him: "Do you think that you are still safe now that Luther's books are burned? Fly and save yourself."

Despite the fact that good people were to be found in both religious groups and nothing was to be gained by becoming a participant in the dispute, Erasmus found himself progressively more irritated and annoyed by Luther's fanaticism and declarations that only his brand of Christianity was true. He could no longer see Luther as only a reformer of abuses. Erasmus recognized the former Augustinian to be a very rebellious person intending to destroy every aspect of the Catholic Church.

Luther, of course, had said this all along. Though Erasmus' desire to keep the peace in hope of reconciliation kept him from seeing Luther in this light, at some point in 1523 or 1524 the former decided that the time had come to take a stand against Luther's more extreme positions. Erasmus hoped to write a tract which would not condemn Luther outright but merely point out the latter's unnecessary extremism and fanaticism. Even

at this late date there was still the possibility of reconciliation, at least a hope.

How could this Dutch satirist debate with the German professor on points of theology when the latter was
infinitely more qualified? Erasmus felt he could not criticize Luther for disregarding Church structure and discipline, for he too had been guilty of this; and attacking
Luther for being critical of all the sacraments would be
hypocritical because his own position also tended to
minimize their importance. The one area however where
Luther appeared to be vulnerable was on the question of
grace and free will, and God's predestination of man;
and while this might have seemed like a secondary issue,
it was actually the most basic point of contention between Luther and his critics. Erasmus was particularly
interested in the entire issue of predestination because
he had built his religious philosophy on man's free will,
or man's ability to act righteously in a spontaneous and
voluntary manner, which Luther denied. If man had no
free will, how could he be pious and make his life on
earth more Godlike? How could man model his life on
that of Christ if he did not have the potential to choose
what he wished to be? To deny free will was to deny the
validity of Erasmus' religious thought; and Luther did
so.

The thrust of Erasmus' criticism of Luther, *Concerning
Free Will*, written in 1524, was to show that if the German professor was correct in his contention that there
was no free will but that all was totally predestined by
God, the natural conclusion would be that accepting or
rejecting Christianity could not effect salvation. First,
Erasmus wrote, if there is predestination then all men
had their lives determined for them by God even before
they were born. If indeed such is the case, and one is
predestined to heaven or to hell, what is the purpose of
Christianity or any religion, and why should man attempt to lead a righteous and religious life if fate will
determine all anyway?

Erasmus continued his attack by asking Luther on what basis might God select some for heaven and others for hell. If such a selection were made on the basis of the conduct of one's life there would be those who were more righteous than others and hence would merit salvation and heaven. If, however, God predetermines man's fate, He must do so on some arbitrary basis without good reason, which would be the height of injustice.

Predestination makes God seem not merely cruel, but a liar as well since He said to the children of Israel they would be rewarded for following Him. Moreover, if all were predetermined, there would have been no need to send Christ to teach man the truth, for mankind would either accept or reject His message on a predetermined basis. Was Christ a liar too when He promised heaven to those that accepted Him as the Son of God, though He must have known that many whom He addressed had no choice but to reject Him? Even more to the point; why would God be so very angry with Adam and Eve for sinning in the Garden of Eden if their sin had been predetermined by Himself? Would God be so very cruel to condemn the very first man to a life of sin? The only logical conclusion was that if evil exists in the world, or if man rejects God, both must be part of God's will and reflect His desires since He has determined all things. This makes God the source of all evil and wickedness in the world.

In Erasmus' mind there was no question that Luther was on the wrong track, for God's greatness lay in His constant efforts to aid man and help him live a more righteous life. The importance of the Ten Commandments, Solomon's Temple, and the coming of Christ, is that each exemplifies God's desire to provide man with enough knowledge to enable man to voluntarily help himself. There could be no doubt that man possessed free will and could choose how he wished to live of his own volition. This was why Adam was chased from Eden, and why some are damned today. On the other hand, those who follow Christ, who are humble, who treat their fellow man with humanity and love will be saved and will be united with God because they have chosen God over the temptations to be uncaring, insincere, and unChristlike. To reject this view was not only absurd to Erasmus, but also made a mockery out of scripture, Christ, and the purpose of Christianity.

Luther's reaction came quickly. In the following year he wrote *The Enslaved Will*, as a reaction and answer to Erasmus' criticism; and while he recognized the validity of the choice of topics, the former aggressively charged: "You know nothing at all of these matters." He denounced Erasmus for writing that some things can never be fully understood, such as predestination, and should therefore not become points of dogma. For Luther all was crystal clear; the "genuine Christian" knew exactly what was true, for the Holy Spirit was no skeptic. The insinuation was that Erasmus was an unbeliever and therefore not a true Christian.

The central problem in Luther's eyes, was not whether God was just or unjust in a human sense, because by His very nature He must be just whether one understands divine justice or not. It was instead whether or not God was omnipotent and omniscient. If the Old Testament account of God were to be accepted, then God's power and will could not be limited. It seemed absurd to Luther that man, corrupted through original sin, might decide on his own to love God when all man's deeds and thoughts are depraved. Even more absurd was the notion that this same man might also involve himself with good works and Christian religious acts, and thereby merit salvation. If such were the case God becomes nothing more than the servant of man, always reacting to man's actions. If man had free will, then God's will was limited as a result.

For Luther, all goodness in man finds its source in God. Man is able to love God; indeed, man first wishes to love God, because God had already infused this individual with grace. If man attains any degree of perfection, he does so not merely because he wishes to be more righteous, but because God has filled him with both the desire and the capacity for goodness. Virtue and reward become the same because those whom God has predestined towards a life of virtue are also those who will merit reward. Moreover, if it was unacceptable to Luther that man might be worthy as a result of his own actions and desires, in such a scheme it might also be unacceptable to suppose that God's grace might be resisted by man. If God wills that even the most miserable sinner is to be saved, it would be an insult to God's glory to suppose that this sinner might not be saved.

Though there is a strong point of logic in Luther's argument, owing to Christianity's constant assumption that God was all knowing and all powerful, Luther showed less interest in an equally important point of Christian belief: that God was all merciful, all forgiving, and all loving. How could one believe that God was all merciful and all loving when He arbitrarily selected some for heaven and damned the rest to hell? One might say with Luther that God's mercy cannot be understood by mortals; but can one disregard all those places where He said man would be rewarded if he voluntarily chose the path of goodness? To a certain extent both Erasmus and Luther accepted the idea that God could not be all knowing, all powerful, all merciful, and all loving at the same time. But where Luther might have preferred to see God as omnipotent and omniscient, for Erasmus the qualities of love and mercy were far more important.

Though it is doubtful that this interchange of ideas altered Erasmus' view of Luther or Lutheranism, the German reformer's lack of humility may have disturbed him. For 1500 years Christians had pondered the correct meaning of scripture, trying to understand how to

improve both Christian belief and practice; yet here was
Luther, comparatively young, with absolutely no doubts
about God's purpose or His self-expression. It had been
this very attitude on the part of some Catholics that had
merited Erasmus' sharpest criticism, causing him to shy
away from the Church. Would he now condone this very
same attitude on Luther's part? Erasmus could well appreciate the young German's enthusiasm, for rebellion
demands great power of conviction; but he could
neither understand nor appreciate the lack of humility
and charity evident in Lutheranism. In 1530 he wrote of
being seriously disturbed by this very quality. "I have
seen them [Lutherans] returning from hearing a sermon, all their faces showing a curious wrath and feroc-
ity as if inspired by an evil spirit." Protestants claimed
they alone understood the Holy Spirit which showed
them the "one true way," but how very often these
words had been used! Every time some fanatic wished
to prove he was right, he said the Holy Spirit had shown
him the only correct interpretation. But how many different opinions could the Holy Spirit entertain, that
everyone claimed such inspiration? Understandably
Erasmus was quite skeptical of such contentions, as he
remarked: "Zwingli and Bucer may be inspired by the
Spirit, Erasmus for himself is nothing but a man and cannot comprehend what is of the spirit."

In addition to his differences with leading Protestants
over questions of faith, free will, and the effectiveness
of the Holy Spirit, there was one area where Erasmus
was certain they had failed completely. With all of their
new institutions and new beliefs, Lutherans were no better Christians than anyone else; nor were they better
human beings. "Just look at the Evangelical [Lutheran]
people; have they become any better? Do they yield less
to luxury, lust, or greed? Show me a man whom the
Gospel has changed . . . I will show you many who have
become even worse than they were." Whatever good the

"drastic surgeon" Luther was accomplishing for Christian thought or practice, he was not producing a very profound effect upon Christian morality or behavior, which for Erasmus was the essence of Christianity. As Erasmus grew old he became more convinced that the seemingly important differences between Catholicism and Lutheranism in reality amounted to little, since both churches had their share of good and bad. He wrote to a friend: "I know that in this church which you call papist [Catholic] there are many who displease me, but I also see such in your church . . . One bears more easily the evils to which one is accustomed. Therefore, I bear with this church until I shall see a better one, and it cannot help bearing with me until I find I shall myself be better. And he does not sail badly who steers a middle course between two evils."

It would be easy to dismiss Erasmus' thoughts as the cynical ramblings of an old and tired man; but to do so is to miss his message, which maintained that piety, goodness, and Christlike behavior are personal characteristics, not elements of belief or church dogma. Because these inspired qualities are to be found neither in the sacraments of the Catholic Church nor in the new practices of the Protestant churches, but rather in the heart of man, the "best" church fails if its members are no more ethical and moral than the members of another church. Erasmus points out that he will stay with the Catholic Church despite its faults until a better one comes along, and quickly adds that the Church will have to bear with him too, for he, like the Church, has faults.

It was unfortunate that people were so divided over issues of belief that separate churches became necessary; but much worse than that, persecution and intolerance were increasing everyday. All about him Erasmus heard the old war cry that persecution was required to root out evil and improper belief. As each side grew more venomous and vindictive, Erasmus declared: "If—what I

say may never happen—you shall see horrible commo-
tions in the word arise . . . then remember Erasmus
prophesied it."

Erasmus lived sufficiently long to see many of his
associates viciously persecuted for their beliefs. In 1535
Thomas More, his closest and oldest friend, was executed by order of Henry VIII of England for rejecting
the idea that the state might determine the true nature
of religion. Erasmus' reaction to all that he saw about
him was weariness, and he prayed "that the Lord might
deign to call [him] out of this raving world to his rest."
In July of 1536 Erasmus, hated by Lutherans, distrusted
by Catholics, died; and in the following years his works
were prohibited by Catholic authorities. His message of
peace and moral goodness would soon be carried away
in the frenzy of international religious war.

After Erasmus' death Protestantism underwent many
internal divisions. John Calvin, the reformer of Geneva,
attempted to establish a Protestant utopia in that city,
and soon the followers of Luther and Calvin were at each
others throats. As Erasmus had predicted, conditions
would get much worse. In the Schmalkaldic wars of the
late 1540's and 1550's, Germany was torn apart by
Catholic and Protestant armies attempting to establish
"the one true religion." These wars proved little except
that neither side could eliminate the other; and not until
1555 was Germany again at peace.

In this year the Peace of Augsburg formally recognized the legitimacy and existence of both Catholic and
Lutheran states; but the seeds of future discontent were
already sown because the treaty did not recognize the
legitimacy of Calvinism, the most militant and expansive
of all the Protestant denominations. Similarly, Anabaptists continued to be persecuted by Protestant and Catholic authorities alike because of the former's pacifism,
communalism, and unwillingness to participate in or
support civil and governmental authority. Erasmus had

come into contact with these small Anabaptist communities; and while he disagreed with their beliefs, still had much good to say about them. "Although this sect is of all the most hated by the princes because of their anarchy and community of goods . . . they defend themselves with no violence . . . In innocence of life they surpass all others. Nevertheless, they are oppressed by the sects [Protestants] as by the orthodox [Catholics]."

After new groups passed through the difficult stages of organization and the founding of a church, they in turn began to persecute their own "heretics" even though just a few years before, every proselyte was greeted with open arms. Strife soon existed not only between Catholic and Protestant, but among the various Protestant groups as well. In time each Reformation denomination would be split into factions, with each asserting that it alone possessed the truth and was the rightful interpreter of the Christian religion.

The strife Erasmus had feared came to pass. Almost every European country was torn by religious dissension and bloody war, with the Holy Spirit the ostensible cause and fierce persecution the predictable result. Luther may have corrected some of the abuses of the Catholic Church; but many forces were unleashed in this process of religious change, and the cost in human life and social peace was very high indeed.

II

THE CONSOLIDATION OF CONFLICT: CALVIN AND RELIGIOUS DISSENT

The success of the Reformation brought Protestantism to ever increasing numbers of people, and the new religion soon developed its own structures, institutions, and in time, its own traditions. One factor of particular importance to the development of Protestantism was the wholesale conversion of many independent city governments; for unlike the small rural parish, a Lutheran city not only provided a base of operations for converting the countryside, but also an opportunity to establish peculiarly Protestant institutions on a large scale. Not surprisingly, in a short time the city became the most important vehicle for spreading the new faith and for experimenting with new institutions.

Despite Erasmus' fears the mood in most Protestant cities was at first quite tolerant. The city represented too many conflicting interests and different sorts of people to move towards the reform too quickly. Lutheranism was preferred to Catholicism, but there were many who could not make this dramatic change in religious life easily. Often monasteries or convents existed on city land, and it proved difficult for older members to give up their Catholic way of life. Many reformed cities like Nuremberg compromised, permitting convents to die out on their own rather than being closed down, as long as they did not recruit new members or interfere with the reform in the city.

This more tolerant mood in the cities can be traced to many other factors. In the early 1520's there was no consistent Protestant point of view which meant that many people held a variety of beliefs. This absence of a new orthodoxy not only permitted great individual latitude but also served as a very important basis for converting disillusioned Catholics who were not quite sure what they believed. Yet another factor for moderation was that many residents of Protestant towns had only recently moved from Catholic areas where they had been persecuted. These immigrants, still unsure of themselves in new surroundings and not certain of what they believed may have had little desire to persecute others, at least not for the time being.

In a very short time, however, all this changed. By the end of the 1530's and beginning of the next decade Protestantism had developed a consistent and far reaching approach to Christianity. Those who in 1520 held no consistent beliefs were now well versed in the new orthodoxy. Members of remaining monasteries or convents had either died or voluntarily moved to Catholic areas. Those Town Councils which in the past were not sure how to deal with new religious responsibility had by this time grown accustomed to their new power and authority. Finally, individuals who fled from persecution a decade before were now well established in their new homes, with the past leaving a bitter memory and perhaps a desire for revenge.

There was at least one additional factor which caused a change in Protestant attitudes from the 1520's to the 1540's. By 1540 it was possible to speak of a second generation of Protestant reformers, who were young enough to have benefited from the many crises and problems facing early Protestantism. This second generation were more sure of their views because they saw the conflict with Catholicism with greater precision and did not have to reach many early conclusions by themselves. Similarly, many were more certain of their ideas, having come to intellectual maturity at the very time Luther broke with the Church. It is also possible that the older generation had spent their energies in making the initial break with the Catholic Church years before, while this newer generation could look forward to expanding and consolidating those gains.

Perhaps the most prominent second generation reformer was John Calvin, born in France in 1509. The son of a notary public, Calvin received an excellent education at the University of Paris where he demonstrated strong ability in literature and law. By 1534 he had converted to Protestantism, and just a few years later in 1538 he wrote the first edition of his famous work, the *Institutes of the Christian Religion*. This early edition was composed of only six chapters, whereas the last edition would have over eighty; but it contained a complete outline of Calvin's thought and the first systematic presentation of Protestant theology.

After deciding to leave France for Protestant Strasbourg Calvin stopped along the way in Geneva in 1538 where Guillaume Farel had just converted the city to Protestantism. When Farel heard that John Calvin, author of the already famous *Institutes*, was in town he begged him to stay in Geneva and help work out a reform program. Calvin hesitated, viewing himself as a scholar and not a man of action, but he finally consented.

Farel and Calvin were somewhat overzealous in attempting to reform Geneva, and two years later they were both exiled because of their moral strictness and what the townspeople saw as an attempt to limit their newly gained freedom. For the next three years Calvin lived in Strasbourg, enlarging his *Institutes* and learning from Martin Bucer, the city's great reformer, how to

bring about change in people's attitudes and institutions. In 1541 he was approached by representatives of
the Genevan Town Council and asked to return to that
city to carry out the reform. After much vacillation
Calvin agreed and remained in Geneva until his death in
1564.

The period of Calvin's residence in Geneva was, generally speaking, a period of intense religious intolerance
throughout Europe; but Calvin earned the reputation of
being one of the most intolerant religious leaders of all.
One historian has written: "If John Calvin ever wrote
anything in favor of religious liberty it was a typographi-
cal error." Even among those who actively supported
him, Calvin was known for his extreme intolerance. If
one man personified all that Erasmus opposed, and if
one city could represent all of Erasmus' fears, it was
John Calvin in Geneva. No reformer showed more zeal
in setting up institutions to organize the lives of average
Christians than he; and few, if any, devoted more time
and energy to suppressing all religious dissent.

The agencies and institutions established by Calvin
covered virtually all aspects of life; but one institution,
the Genevan Consistory, is of special importance. This
public body, composed of the ministers of the churches
and representatives of the community, acted on problems of morals and church discipline. The Consistory
received its information from agents throughout the
city, who made reports on their districts. By today's
standards the punishments meted out by this court seem
very harsh; an adultress was bound up in a sack and
dropped into a river, and homosexuals were decapitated.
The Consistory also had the power to excommunicate
any resident of Geneva, which meant it could cut someone off from all aspects of social life. Needless to say,
such a tool could be of immense value in controlling the
opinions and actions of those living in the city. For
instance, one Town Councilman, Phillip Berthelier, was

excommunicated by Calvin for being too jolly and frivo-
lous at a wedding reception. Some people undoubtedly
felt that such immoral behavior had to be checked by
severe punishment, but others pointed out that Berthelier might have received such strict punishment because
he was one of the Town Council's leading opponents to
Calvin's plans. In all fairness it should be pointed out
that Geneva was not unique in having such an institution as the Consistory; but while most Protestant towns
had such a body of people, in no other town did it have
so much power or use it so freely.

Though there were many incidents and clashes between Calvin and others in Geneva over religious issues,
perhaps none typify his attitude more clearly than the
cases of Jerome Bolsec and Michael Servetus. These two
cases constitute exactly the kind of situation Erasmus
feared most. They are examples of repression of religious dissent and of great power misused, ostensibly for
the greater glory of God. It is therefore worthwhile to
discuss them in some detail, not because of their unique-
ness but rather because they exemplify the kind of
events that were taking place throughout Europe.

Jerome Bolsec, an ex-Carmelite monk and Protestant
refugee from France, had in 1550 settled at Vigny near
Geneva, as the personal physician to a Protestant noble-
man. Because of his past interest in theology he often
attended the weekly meetings of Genevan ministers,
when scripture and religious issues were discussed. At
one such meeting in 1551 one minister explained a difficult Biblical passage and how it supported Calvin's view
of predestination. Bolsec then rose and criticized Calvin's predestinarian views, stating that such opinions
made God into a tyrant and the source of all evil. In
short, Bolsec, like Erasmus, claimed predestination was
totally incorrect.

Calvin was so incensed at Bolsec's audacity that upon
the former's request, the Town Council threw the ex-

monk into jail after which he was charged with heresy.
A trial soon followed with Calvin demanding that Bolsec
be executed for denying predestination. The Town
Council members, who did not know what to make of
such complicated views and issues or whether execution
was a fitting punishment, could come to no conclusion.
It was therefore determined that the best course of action would be to consult the other Swiss Churches for
their opinions. When the answers appeared, Calvin
found them uniformly unsatisfactory. Bern replied that
the whole issue was such a mystery that men should not
fight over it; and Basle and Zurich would give Calvin
only very qualified support, with the latter city critical
of the way the case had been handled. Only Farel's
Neuchâtel gave Calvin an unqualified endorsement. The
Genevan Town Council's decision was to banish Bolsec
from Geneva, less because of the heresy charge than in
order to keep the peace in the city. The Bolsec case
ended as a partial victory for Calvin; for though Bolsec
had not been executed, denial of even a mysterious concept like predestination proved adequate grounds for
prosecution.

Had the Bolsec affair been simply an isolated instance
of Calvin's uncompromising attitude, one might be
tempted to overlook it as just one more example of
sixteenth century intolerance. But only two years later
Calvin went to even greater lengths to crush another
divergent view.

Michael Servetus was born in 1509 in Villanueva,
Spain. In 1531 at the age of 22 he published his first
work, *Concerning the Errors of the Trinity*, in which he
boldly attacked the conventional views and opinions of
Christianity's most basic doctrine. He did not deny the
existence of the Father, Son, or the Holy Spirit, but
simply maintained that for approximately 1200 years
Christians had not understood the proper relationship
between these three divine personalities, a fault he was

prepared to correct. In the following year he wrote another work, *Dialogues on the Trinity*, in which he reiterated his views. Although many authors in the past had criticized traditional formulations of the trinity, none were as bold as Servetus in demonstrating how this view had no basis in scripture and how it was the product of a faulty tradition in Christian history. Moreover, the latter maintained that Protestants were no better than Catholics on this point, perhaps even worse, and so brought upon himself the wrath and hatred of both Catholics and Protestants. Wisely, Servetus assumed the alias Michael Villanovanus since it was not prudent to use his real name anywhere in Europe.

Over the next twenty years Servetus moved from one city to the next, changing occupations all the while and succeeding at whatever he did. He edited the traditional text on geography in such a way that some claim he laid the basis for comparative geography and demography. He studied medicine at the University of Paris and wrote tracts ranging in subjects from digestive juices to syphilis. Some medical authorities even claim that Servetus was the first to discover the pulmonary circulation of the blood. Not all his efforts, however, were strictly scientific. He wrote a tract defending "judicial astrology," or fortune telling, and edited a multilingual translation of the Bible adding his own introduction, which contained many revolutionary ideas about the nature of prophecy.

In 1546 Servetus began a correspondence with Calvin and sent him a manuscript of an as yet unpublished work, *The Restitution of Christianity*, which was even more extreme and heretical than anything he had written to that time. Servetus not only denied the trinity, but he accepted pantheistic ideas about God's nature, and expressed a belief that man could be deified just as Christ had passed from being mortal to divine. After receiving several letters Calvin grew angry with the

ravings and rantings of what appeared to him to be a
madman, and wrote to his friend Farel that if Servetus
ever stepped into Geneva he would never leave alive.
Possibly towards this end Calvin kept Servetus' manuscript and letters though the author had asked for their
return.

About 1552 Dr. Michael Villanovanus, personal
physician to the Archbishop of Vienne, was discovered
to be the infamous and devilish Michael Servetus. A
Genevan resident and friend of Calvin's, Guillaume de
Trye, wrote to his Catholic cousin in Lyon, France that
Villanovanus was Servetus and included with his letter
some of the correspondence that had passed between
Calvin and Servetus. It has long been suspected that
Calvin was behind the plot to uncover Servetus because
de Trye, writing from Geneva, was able to supply docu-
ments only in Calvin's possession. In a very short time
Servetus was called to face charges of heresy in the in-
quisitors' court in Lyon. Fortunately for Servetus he was
able to escape from jail during the trial, leaving the
Catholic authorities to be content with burning him in
effigy.

For some unknown reason Servetus headed for
Geneva though he must have realized that Calvin had
supplied the incriminating evidence against him. Some
historians contend that Servetus meant only to pass
through Geneva on his way to southern Italy because
once in Geneva, he attempted to keep his identity a
secret. In spite of his precautions, however, Calvin's followers discovered his presence and brought about his
incarceration on various heresy charges. From August
14 to October 25, 1553, Servetus stood trial for thirty-
eight charges of heresy, with Calvin acting as prosecutor
throughout most of the proceedings. In this case as in
the Bolsec affair, the Town Council did not know quite
what to make of most of the testimony. Calvin and

Servetus took turns shouting at each other and taunting the other with provocative questions. Though it was very clear that Servetus was indeed a terrible heretic, no one was exactly sure what his views were or what Calvin was saying for that matter, because the discussion was much too deep for this group of Councilmen. On several occasions Servetus was questioned by representatives of the pastors in Geneva, but they received little more satisfaction from him than did Calvin. Once again the Town Council was presented with the demand that this heretic be executed, and once again they felt it would be prudent to seek the advice of the other churches in Switzerland. To avoid the bitter experience of two years earlier Calvin also wrote to these churches, explaining his position and why Servetus ought to be found guilty and executed. Within a short time the Swiss churches answered to Calvin's satisfaction; all agreed that Servetus should be condemned. The Town Council set a date of execution, and on October 17, 1553, Michael Servetus was burnt alive at the stake, over green wood to prolong his agony. It took the poor man a full half hour to die.

Servetus was not the first heretic to be burnt at the stake, yet his death caused a sensation all over Europe. Very few people defended Servetus' views, but many for a variety of reasons were shocked by his death. Some were disturbed that Servetus should have been brought to trial without having committed any overt act of heresy in Geneva. If Servetus could be executed for the views he held in his heart, who then was safe from the executioner? Still others felt that Servetus should have been exiled from Geneva, much as Bolsec had, even if he was a terrible heretic. Quite possibly Protestants more than Catholics were disturbed by Calvin's actions because many of them had left Catholicism through considerations of conscience. Moreover, were there not

Protestants all over Europe who protested against
Catholic treatment of French Protestants on the basis of
freedom of conscience?

Still others were troubled by the old issue of predestination. If Calvin was correct in his assumptions about
predestination, should a harmless heretic like Servetus
have been put to death? If the reprobate and the elect
had already been chosen by God what effect could Servetus have had? It was also asked: If Calvin's actions
were predestined by God, did this not reduce religion to
the level of legalized and institutionalized murder? More
than anything else, Servetus' execution provoked the
question: Was all this really Christ's intent? Had He indeed been crucified for this?

Erasmus' warnings of what the future would bring
had clearly gone unheeded for a number of years, as
most people simply adjusted to the increasing level of
persecution and intolerance. Although there were always those who opposed persecution in the name of
Christ, the same divisive voices which had disregarded
Erasmus ignored those who initially opposed Calvin.
The Bolsec and Servetus affairs, however, provoked a
reaction from many who had been silent all along but
who now felt that things had gone too far. In Geneva
the reaction to Servetus' death was relatively mild because Calvin was held in high regard, and most had
grown accustomed to trusting his judgment. But outside
Geneva, in Basle and Germany, there was growing criticism of Calvin's actions.

To combat this emerging concern about Servetus'
execution, Calvin decided to write an explanation of his
actions by presenting the religious basis for the persecution of heretics. This work, *A Defense of the Orthodox
Faith Against the Prodigious Errors of the Spaniard
Michael Servetus*, was published less than half a year
after Servetus' death, and has been described by one
historian as "one of the most frightening treatises ever

written to justify the persecution of heretics." The major theme which runs throughout the work, is that those who blaspheme the glory of God must be punished; and to this end no action is too extreme or too inhumane. Indeed, Calvin writes: "One should forget all mankind when His glory is in question," and to insult the glory of God is worse than strangling someone or even poisoning your guests. Any type of persecution was acceptable as long as one "did not tolerate that God's name be reviled."

Contemporaries pointed out Calvin's fallacious logic in condemning the Catholic Church's persecution of French Calvinists when he himself laid such a careful basis for persecution and had already acquired a reputation for intolerance. Calvin's answer however was that Protestants, Calvinists in particular, had the right to persecute whom they willed because they were right; and Catholics could not persecute Protestants because the former were wrong. Simply put, Calvin felt he alone spoke for God.

This rather extreme treatise was criticized from the outset. Nicholas Zurkinden, the Secretary of State of the Bern city government, saw one of the first copies printed and was moved to write to Calvin: "More than once you have seemed to me too rigid and too harsh, and I have freely told you so. It is true that I in turn seem too kind and easy going to you; but I prefer to sin this way rather than fall into the opposite extreme." Zurkinden, a highly respected individual in Switzerland and one of Calvin's strong supporters in most instances, went on to say: "I saw with my own eyes a woman, eighty years old, and her daughter, a mother of six children now orphans, dragged to the place of execution for the single crime of having refused to have the children baptised according to the known teaching and customs . . . . " Indeed, tens of thousands of Anabaptists were persecuted throughout Europe in these years.

Zurkinden's letter was more of an attempt at friendly persuasion than outright criticism or condemnation, but there were those who did condemn Calvin openly and completely. Within a month of Servetus' death the Swiss churches received scores of letters from important people who felt Calvin had been much too harsh; and after publication of his defense the reaction was much the same. In fact, it is very possible that in the long run Calvin's work hurt his cause much more than it helped. Through Calvin, Servetus' views reached a very large audience; and the former was forced into the unenviable position of having to defend such a negative practice as persecution, a very difficult task. Among those who felt Calvin to be wrong was Sebastian Castellio, a man who would devote the rest of his life to combatting religious persecution in general, and the Genevan reformer in particular.

Castellio, born in 1515 in the village of Bresse about thirty-five miles west of Geneva, was educated at the University of Lyon, where he established a reputation as a first-rate classical scholar. Like many others who were bothered by the Catholic Church's apparent inability to reform itself and its overemphasis on external ritual, he left for Protestant Strasbourg where he converted to Protestantism. It was at this time that Calvin was exiled from Geneva and began to head for Strasbourg, where these two scholars were to strike up a very close friendship. When Calvin returned to Geneva three years later, he took Castellio with him to be rector of a new Calvinist college that the former was planning. Castellio loved his work and was extremely competent but was unable to make ends meet on the low salary the position paid. Not wishing to lose such a valuable man, the Town Council advised the rector to apply for the ministry to augment his income; but when he requested a ministerial position, his application was rejected by Calvin. The two could not agree about the exact nature of Christ's descent into hell and the real meaning of the *Song of Songs*, while Calvin had come to have misgivings about Castellio's independent mind. His rejection is difficult to understand in light of the fact that several Genevan ministers who were leading immoral lives and were "financially irresponsible" received no criticism from Calvin, nor were they rejected by the ministry. Disappointed, Castellio left Geneva for Basle in 1544 where he and his family lived in total poverty for the next eight years. He attempted to earn a living by correcting publishers' proofs and through teaching, but it seems the only work he could find was carrying water for gardeners and harpooning drifting logs on the Rhine river. To keep his family from actual starvation he had to become a fisherman.

During these lean years Castellio succeeded in completing a long-term project, a correct Latin and simple French translation of the Bible, which was finally published in 1551. The preface of the Bible edition was dedicated to King Edward VI of England, and expressed for the first time Castellio's deep feelings about religious persecution and the sorry state of religion because of gross intolerance. "What times do we live in? . . . We are becoming bloodthirsty killers out of zeal for Christ . . . out of zeal for Christ we persecute others!" To persecute another for "wrong" religious opinions is to presume to know how God reacts to such views, which is both foolish and presumptive on man's part. "Let us await the sentence of the just judge, and let us take care not to condemn others and not do anything for which we should be afraid of being condemned." It is not known whether Castellio directed this barb at Calvin, for the Bolsec case was then current; but Calvin interpreted this preface to be referring to him; and from this point onward he and Castellio were on very poor terms.

In 1553, the year of Servetus' death, Castellio's luck changed, as he was appointed professor of Greek at the

University of Basle. Though he was a popular teacher, Calvin and his associate, Theodore Beza, urged the Basle Town Council to fire Castellio and prosecute him as a dangerous enemy of the true religion. It was at this point in their strained relationship that Servetus' execution disturbed the peace of Switzerland and prompted Castellio to feel the need to attack Calvin's actions and to arouse some movement of criticism against intolerance and high-handed persecution.

Castellio's first treatise on toleration, *Concerning Heretics and Whether They Should be Punished by Magistrates*, was less a personal attack upon Calvin than a general condemnation and refutation of the religious basis of persecution and intolerance. From the very first pages the author states that the essence of Christianity lay in the quality of one's moral and ethical life rather than in the exactness or accuracy of doctrine. Indeed, Castellio points out that where Christians have become too preoccupied with the exact meaning of difficult doctrines, they tend to forget ethics and morality altogether, making persecution not only possible, but theoretically necessary. To illustrate how very foolish religious intolerance is, Castellio presents the reader with a parable where a prince is about to leave his domain on a long trip. Up till his time of departure the prince's subjects had lived truly moral lives, as he wanted them to. Upon leaving the one request the good prince makes is that while he is away all should continue living good moral and ethical lives, not fighting with one another until he returns and has the opportunity to resolve all arising disputes.

However, as soon as the prince departs, all his subjects begin attacking one another as being unfaithful to him and not remembering him the way one ought. Soon the population of the manor is split into various groups and factions, each claiming that it alone remembers the prince and therefore represents him. Rather than acting with charity towards each other, each faction condemns the others because they differ about where the prince was at that exact moment, precisely when he would return, and how he would look and what kind of horse he would be riding. In short, the prince's subjects were doing everything he had requested they not do, and ostensibly in his name.

For Castellio Christ was the departing prince who made abundantly clear through the Sermon on the Mount, His parables, and sayings that He wished men to lead moral and ethical lives. But what do Christians argue about? Did Christ descend into hell or is He at the right hand of God? Would Christ return in the near future or only after a millennium? Would He come on a great cloud or as a humble man? The author reasoned that Christ could not have been terribly interested in such issues because His actions in this world were not directed towards analytical exactness of doctrine but towards moral perfection. Moreover, those beliefs and practices which are necessary for salvation are clearly explained in the Bible, for it was not Christ's nature to hold man responsible for difficult views and esoteric practices not clearly explained.

Yet how did Castellio see conditions in his own time? Those persons wishing to lead a moral life and not embroil themselves in controversy over difficult dogmas are persecuted in the name of Christ. "All sects hold their religion according to the Word of God and say that it is certain. Calvin says that he is certain. He says they are wrong and wishes to be judge, and so do they. Who shall be judge? Who made Calvin the arbiter of all the sects that he alone should kill? He has the Word of God as have they. If the matter is certain, to whom is it certain? To Calvin? But why then does he write so many books about manifest truth?"

Not only Calvin but virtually every other sectarian leader saw Castellio as a dangerous man since they were

all certain that they alone knew the truth. They therefore felt bound to eliminate all other views even if this
meant waging a war of extermination. Castellio prophesied: "Calvin would have to invade France and other
nations, wipe out cities, put all the inhabitants to the
sword sparing neither sex nor age, not even the babes
and the beasts."

Under such conditions someone of "true" faith in one
town would be considered a heretic in another. "If in
this city or region you are considered a true member of
the faithful, next door you will be looked upon as a
heretic, so much so, that if one wishes to live today one
needs as many faiths and religions as there are cities or
sects." Being a heretic is reduced to holding the wrong
view in the wrong place. To Castellio the "true Christian" could of course avoid all such difficulties by never
leaving his town and preferably never leaving his house.
He ends his preface with a plea to Christ: "If thou dost
wish those things and orderest them to be done, what
hast thou left to the devil to do?"

The reaction to the book was immediate. Theodore
Beza, Calvin's associate in Geneva, wrote to Bullinger,
the most important minister in Basle: "If what he has
spewed out in his preface is to be endured, what, pray,
have we left of the Christian religion? The doctrines of
the office of Christ, the trinity, the Lord's supper, bap-
tism, justification, free will, the state of the soul after
death, are either useless or at least not necessary for
salvation. No one is to be condemned as a heretic. You
see what this leads to?" Indeed, Beza was so agitated
that with Calvin's permission he wrote a refutation of
Castellio's views called *Concerning the Punishment of
Heretics by Civil Magistrates.* The main thrust of Beza's
opus is simple. No crime is as great as heresy and no
punishment too severe: " . . . what greater crime could
one find among men? Surely if one wanted to prescribe
a punishment according to the greatness of the crime it

would be impossible to find a torture big enough to fit the enormity of such a misdeed." Beza was simply echoing Calvin's views.

Castellio would not let the issue drop now that it was attracting real attention. Religious toleration was not simply one more dogma accepted or rejected but the very fiber of Christian morality; and since it was useless to argue with Beza, in 1554 Castellio wrote another treatise entitled *Against Calvin's Book*. In format it is a point by point refutation of Calvin's views, as the name implies, with Castellio's arguments following the same pattern as that of his earlier writings.

While Christianity is both doctrinal and moral the moral aspect, according to Castellio, is clear and easy to follow whereas the doctrinal elements are often vague or difficult to understand. Therefore, great latitude should be applied in relation to dogma. Since every man is responsible for his own salvation, the various religious sects should require uniformly high ethical standards but should also permit each man to believe as he wishes within very wide limits. Since the Bible is too vague on many issues, there should be no persecution of minority opinions. Moreover, the truth cannot be known in this life, and intolerance is immoral in a Christian context. Although the magistrate or city official is responsible for keeping the peace in his town, he should not be an arbiter of religious truth because that role has nothing to do with keeping the peace. Castellio added: "Killing a man is not defending a doctrine, it is merely killing a man. When the people of Geneva killed Servetus they did not defend a doctrine, they killed a man. It is not the magistrates' business to defend doctrines . . . If Servetus had wanted to kill Calvin, the magistrate would have been fully entitled to defend Calvin. But since Servetus only fought with writing and arguments, he should have been rebutted with writings and arguments."

Though this work was widely circulated in manu-

script, it was published only in 1612, partially because
Calvin successfully attempted to keep Castellio's treatise
from wide circulation and partially because many publishers were afraid of putting Castellio into print lest
there be repercussions against their company. Although
Castellio was well known all over Europe and many ap-
provingly read his defences of religious toleration, he
nevertheless had almost no effect on the policies of
rulers or religious leaders of his time.

While specific reasons for this lack of success are
many and self evident, there are at least two long stand-
ing factors which contributed to Castellio's failure.
First, the antagonism that had been generated between
Catholic and Protestant was still so strong that accepting
a liberal tolerationist position was equated with religious
treason. Second, in times of great popular enthusiasm,
belief often gravitates towards extremism. Just as Erasmus, perhaps the most popular author of his day, could
not influence the course of his times because of widespread demands for instant reform with no consideration of the practical problems involved; so too in Castellio's era, a generation after Erasmus, the emotional
nature of religious issues obliterated any chance for
peaceful coexistence.

III

THE INTENSIFICATION OF CONFLICT: RESISTANCE, REGICIDE, SKEPTICISM

In attempting to determine why post-Reformation Christians could not readily perceive the utter futility of religious fanaticism, intolerance, and persecution, it might be instructive to focus upon what could be called the two matrices of strife evident in sixteenth century Europe. The first was characterized by conflict, engendered through the habitual unwillingness of most religious institutions and denominations to maintain peaceful coexistence. The second, by violence arising from the reluctance of the major, yet essentially weak, secular institutions to maintain peace.

The religious leaders of the late sixteenth century might well have been expected to grow tired of continued crisis and protracted bloodletting, but just the opposite was the case. In the period between 1570 and 1610, as in previous periods, the leaders of religious denominations stood at the forefront of any attempt to divide Europe. Each group continued to believe that it alone represented Christ, and that all the rest were agents of the devil, bound for hell. In 1576, two decades after peace had been restored to Germany, the Calvinist professor Jerome Zanchi of the University of Heidelberg tried to provoke princes into renewed fanaticism by requesting they rescind Catholic rights: "The devout prince must not, and indeed cannot in

conscience, allow his Catholic subjects in his territory to
have churches for the practice of their idolatrous worship and the preaching of heretical doctrine. He should
rather . . . destroy these churches with their idols and
false worship." For their part Catholic leaders were no
better as they demanded that princes try Protestants in
courts of inquisition on charges of heresy, and that Protestant churches be destroyed.

Similarly, the divisions between the various Protestant sects continued to grow and harden. Calvinists
showed contempt for Lutheran willingness to retain
minor points of Catholic ritual and tradition, and
Lutherans saw Calvinists as dangerous radicals and mad-
men, bent on obliterating all church tradition. Lutheran
writings abound with terms like "diabolical Calvinists,"
"satanic brood of Calvin," and other pejorative descrip-
tions, which illustrate the growing alienation of these
two groups. One Lutheran minister wrote in 1615: "As
long as the Calvinists are not in power, and as long as
they are obliged to submit to the existing authority,
they are pleasant and patient . . . but as soon as they are
master of the situation they will not tolerate a single
syllable of Lutheran doctrine. Everything must be abol-
ished . . . ." Indeed, the hatred between these two Protestant groups was so great that by the turn of the
seventeenth century a Lutheran minister felt that "on
the whole there is more common ground between Catholics and the followers of Luther than between the latter and the Calvinists."

The differences between these two denominations
had been developing for many years. During the very
early years of the Reformation, German Protestants and
Swiss Reformed churches were sufficiently similar in
thinking and orientation to facilitate the formation of a
united front against a powerful Catholic Church. In
time, however, Lutherans and Calvinists found progressively more about which to disagree. The basic point of

contention centered around the meaning of the Eucharist. While both churches agreed that the Catholic practices were incorrect and that the cup as well as the wafer must be administered to the communicant, they could not agree on the meaning of the ritual itself. As early as 1529 German and Swiss theologians reluctantly met in Marburg in a halfhearted attempt to work out the sticky details of this major dogma. The Eucharist was an issue of vital importance because it was one of the two sacraments Protestants continued to accept. Moreover, it was believed to represent the link between man and Christ, and man and his Church.

Luther believed that Christ was physically in the Eucharist, as indeed He was everywhere. Receiving the Eucharist had profound religious meaning because it united the believer with Christ and the Church, through which the sacrament was administered. The Swiss churches, represented at this early date by Zwingli, accepted a very different position. For them the Eucharist was more of a commemorative act signifying the believer's personal identification with his Church and its beliefs. Because Christ was not physically in the Eucharist, this ritual had no profound religious meaning. Furthermore, the position of the Church was not exalted because nothing supernatural occurred. The conflict did not erupt into a serious breach, in part because Calvin was able to convince many former Zwinglians to espouse a position more conciliatory to Lutheran views. For a time the issue seemed resolved with both sides accepting that Christ was somehow in the Eucharist, and that there was some sort of religious meaning to the act.

To ensure that this potentially explosive issue would not cause a rift between Germans and Swiss, Luther's associate, Philipp Melanchthon, published in 1540 a variation of the accepted list of Lutheran beliefs. While this new confession did much to forestall a possible breach between Lutherans and Calvinists, it angered

more conservative Lutherans who felt convinced that
Melanchthon was selling out to the Calvinists. Luther
himself seems to have been unhappy with Melanchthon's formulations and expressed his own doubts. Unfortunately, Luther died a few years later leaving his
church split into pro- and anti-Melanchthon groups.

By 1552 Melanchthon's honest attempts at reconciliation gave way to open disagreement between the Germans and Swiss. In that year a major Lutheran theologian, Joachim Westfal, wrote a book attacking both
Calvin and Bullinger. As a result, when Calvin visited
Frankfort in 1556 it was observed that he got along
poorly with resident Lutheran ministers. With no major
Lutherans or Calvinists attempting to maintain the pre-
carious peace, the Eucharist controversy surfaced, destroying whatever mutual toleration these churches had
exhibited in the past.

Indeed, other issues which might separate the Protestant and the Reformed churches began to emerge. While
Melanchthon may have been closer to Calvin than German theologians on the Eucharist; when it came to predestination, or ideas on the incarnation, the German-
Swiss breach was very great.

In the following years both denominations developed
along their own lines with little or no attempt to work
out common Protestant confessions. In 1577 the German churches agreed to a list of beliefs separate from a
confession accepted by the Swiss in 1566.

This rising inter-denominational antagonism was not
helped by Lutheran-Calvinist competition for converts
in the Holy Roman Empire. According to the terms of
the Peace of Augsburg of 1555, ruling princes had the
option of choosing either Lutheranism or Catholicism,
but not Calvinism. The latter were less than pleased with
this development and proceeded to make converts not
only in areas still Catholic, but in Lutheran regions as
well. The best example of such inter-denominational

competition was the Palatinate. In the course of sixty years this single German state had left the Catholic Church, twice accepted Lutheran belief and practice only to give them up as many times in order to embrace Calvinism. Such confrontations consolidated and crystallized the ill will that had existed over doctrinal issues. The religious map of Europe was further complicated by internal divisions within the major denominations themselves. It has been pointed out how Lutherans were soon divided into "Philippists" and anti-"Philippists" known as Flacians. Similarly, Calvinism was split into different warring parties. In Holland about 1600 the leading Protestant church was Calvinist, but it contained two major branches which detested each other. One group accepted and further developed Calvin's views concerning predestination, and had the support of Theodore Beza, Calvin's heir. The second group attempted to modify these views into a more humane religious context. In 1611 at the Council of Dort, an international meeting of Calvinist churches, resolutions were drawn up supporting the predestinarian group and thereby causing a total split in the Dutch church. In the following twenty years the losing group was subject to the worst type of harassment and persecution at the hands of their fellow Calvinists. Religious peace and toleration could have been brought about had each denomination or faction assumed an enlightened position regarding other religious groups.

A second factor leading to war and conflict in the sixteenth century was the inability or unwillingness of secular governments to forcefully restore peace despite the desires of religious organizations. Throughout the Middle Ages the central government and king often had very limited powers. Feudalism and manorialism were decentralized systems of social organization where each feudal lord provided governmental services on a local level. While the king might determine some aspects of

foreign policy, day to day governance of the realm fell
to the local lord. The one genuinely unifying social institution was the Catholic Church, functioning through its
bureaucratic hierarchy and network of monasteries,
nunneries, and ecclesiastical institutions. The fourteenth
century brought an end to this static situation when
monarchs all over Europe attempted to consolidate their
power through the creation of viable central governments. These new policies brought the king into conflict
with the noble class, which almost axiomatically possessed the real wealth of the realm, and with the
Church, whose position had remained stable partially as
a result of the instability of royal-noble relations.

While the decentralized feudal class was easily divided
and conquered, the Church posed a different problem to
the monarch because it was international in scope and
could count on the support of its allies all across Europe. Yet even in this case, the royal government
emerged victorious. The classic encounter between King
and Church came when Philip the Fair of France attempted to tax ecclesiastical holdings in his realm. When
the Church vigorously remonstrated, Philip simply neutralized its power by kidnapping and indirectly killing
the Pope, after which he virtually brought about the
imprisonment of the Papacy on French soil for the next
seventy years.

By the time of the Reformation most kings in Europe
had so enormously strengthened their position in relation to the noble classes that they were ready to review
their entire relationship and ties with the Church. In
1516 the king of France and the Papacy agreed to the
Concordat of Bologna, which accorded the French national Church a fair degree of self autonomy, while His
Most Christian Majesty was granted a strong measure of
control over indigenous church institutions. In 1534
King Henry VIII of England found it necessary for reasons of state to institute a national English Catholic

Church, Catholic in religion but English and royal in authority and control. In Spain the Catholic monarchs, Ferdinand and Isabella, instituted the redoubtable Spanish Inquisition, which served the double role of suppressing any and all tendencies towards heresy, and acting as a battering ram to demolish every threat to the newly unified country.

All over Europe religion was being used by centralizing monarchs in an attempt to crush rebellious religious and political forces. It was in recognition of the monarch's importance that the Peace of Augsburg based religious determination on the prince's will rather than on any other agency. Logically this should have brought peace to all Europe because each prince had some religious preference. In reality, instead of bringing peace, making religion a function of the royal will further escalated the violence. Because each prince was of such importance, the competition between Protestantism and Catholicism to convert them grew very intense.

Moreover, it raised problems of crucial significance. What might happen, for instance, when an important prince was converted to the "wrong" religion, or if he refused to convert to the "right" religion? Many religious thinkers felt that in such a case the only course of action was deposition, or if need be, assassination. But what would happen if the prince could not be assassinated? Did his subjects have the right to resist his policies though he was the divinely appointed ruler of that territorial unit?

It is not suprising that in the period after 1555 both Protestants and Catholics developed theories of resistance and regicide. If the problems of a religiously divided Europe could not be solved through local conversion, nor through war, then only assassination and rebellion remained.

Theories of active resistance against a legitimate authority go back to the Middle Ages, when a vassal might bring his feudal lord before a council of the latter's own peers for violating some aspect of their contractual relationship. In almost all cases the basis of this resistance was legal in nature—that is, one of the parties involved had not fulfilled his responsibilities as delineated in a feudal charter, or had assumed too much authority and was therefore usurping power. Because it was often difficult to determine the exact legal point under contention, or who should bear major responsibility, many such disputes were resolved on the field of battle rather than in a court of law.

In the Holy Roman Empire, a loose confederation of separate German principalities, the princes and the Emperor were continually at odds about the limits of princely sovereignty or the extent of imperial power. While this conflict had been festering for decades before Luther, the Reformation added one more dimension to it and provided yet another reason for resisting legitimate authority: the maintainance of the true faith. The Schmalkaldic wars, fought for many deeply rooted political and economic reasons, were justified on both sides by religious arguments.

In the period after the Peace of Augsburg writings dealing with the rights of religious resistance continued to be read by an ever-increasing audience. Most tracts concerned with political resistance, however, recognized that not every person had the right to rebel. Generally, this right (or duty) was limited to governmental institutions such as representative assemblies, Parliaments, or royal commissions. Such institutions were an integral part of the government of a given country and therefore shared with the prince the aura of divine sanction. Similarly, those of the prince's bloodline also possessed the rights of resistance because they too were of the royal family, chosen by God to rule.

Yet another agency of government that might actively resist higher authority according to Protestant thinkers was the Town Council of a legitimate city government. Though this type of elected government was fundamentally unlike that of a monarchy, Protestant thinkers in particular drew parallels between the rights of a prince and those of the Town Council because many such governments were Lutheran or Calvinist and indeed had resisted Charles V.

The problems facing Catholic theoreticians were somewhat different from those that beset the Protestants. If in the early years of the Reformation the latter were interested in overturning legitimate government, the former were concerned with suppressing resistance and rebellion. If Protestants claimed that rebellion might be permissible by some agencies of government to introduce the "proper faith," Catholics argued that maintenance of the "true faith" justified the most harsh and cruel suppression. Rather than concentrating on those governmental agencies permitted to resist legitimate authority, Catholic lawyers concentrated upon the central position of the Papacy in recognizing and sanctioning legitimate government. Catholic treatises saw the coronation ceremony as the outward sign of a religious contract between the prince and God, where the former promised to maintain the true faith. In this ceremony the prince received God's permission to rule, in being anointed by His regent, the Pope, or an archbishop. He retained God's support only as long as he accepted papal religious leadership.

Any prince who broke this contract by converting to Protestantism, could no longer rule or be considered a legitimate authority. The agency to determine whether a prince had indeed violated his contract was the Pope, who might declare any such prince a tyrant, or a usurper of power. In such cases the king's Catholic subjects possessed the right to resist him not merely because he might be a heretic, but also because the Pope had declared him to be an enemy of God. Theoretically all such rulers would abdicate. This of course never happened.

What power did the Pope possess to force the abdication of a recalcitrant prince? Some thinkers, like Robert Bellarmine, claimed the Pope only possessed the power to declare a king illegitimate, while actual deposition was a local matter to be dealt with by the king's subjects. Some continued Bellarmine's train of thought, asserting that only local Catholic officials might depose a king, declared a tyrant or a usurper of power, no matter how obnoxious he proved to be in God's eyes. Others, however, argued that the Pope might exert a more direct influence, perhaps even raise an army and call a crusade against the heretical king. Indeed, Sixtus V, Pope in 1588 at the time of the Spanish Armada's attack on England, bestowed his Godly blessing upon this attempt to depose Elizabeth I. Other Popes attempted to intervene by utilizing other methods such as that of excommunication; and both Elizabeth I and Henry of Navarre were thus separated from all Catholic graces and blessings. In both cases Catholic subjects were urged to rebel against all excommunicated "tyrants," thereby placing the former in the unfortunate position of betraying either their king or their God. Those who chose God faced a charge of treason and possible execution; while those who opted for their secular ruler risked eternal damnation (so they were told in any event by their parish priests).

Whatever the differences between Protestant and Catholic thinking, Protestant resistance proved more effective in reality. In basing their theories on the Papacy, Catholic thinking was compact and to the point; but it did not create any body or agency which might bring about the change the Pope desired. On the other hand, Protestant thinking based itself on the reality of municipal willingness to participate in rebellion. Had the Pope been able to raise armies or convince

Catholic kings of the need for a crusade, Catholic theories of resistance would have been much more effective. However, not to be outdone by Protestant violence, the Papacy was able to circumvent its apparent lack of effectiveness. Rather than relying on the possibility of a Catholic rebellion, its loyal Jesuit thinkers presented the advantages of assassination or regicide. Assassination has always possessed many "virtues" because of its organizational manageability. Moreover, inexpensive professional assassins or simply fanatics were not difficult to find; and if successful, yielded excellent results. Finally, if one attempt failed, another could just as easily be organized. Some Jesuits like Immanuel Sâ considered murdering a tyrant an "absolute duty." The German Catholic professor Adam Turner wished to make clear to Protestant rulers that "they should be convinced that one has not only a perfect right to kill them [tyrants], but that to accomplish such a deed is glorious and heroic." It was the Jesuit theologian Suarez, however, who put it most succinctly: "It is an article of faith that the Pope has the right to depose heretical and rebellious kings; and a monarch dethroned by the Pope is no longer a king or a legitimate ruler. When such a king hesitates to obey the Pope after he is deposed he then becomes a tyrant and may be killed by the first comer. Especially when the public good is assured by the death of the tyrant it is allowable for anyone to kill the latter." These were neither idle threats nor empty words. In the years between 1570 and 1600 important Protestant leaders experienced numerous, often successful, attempts on their lives.

Protestants too developed theories of regicide. Based on their religious concept of the "calling" where every person was envisioned as having a specific role to fill in this world, determined through God's predestination, Protestant thinkers claimed that some were called by God to be assassins, as others were called to be ministers or blacksmiths. This too was not vacuous theorizing, for many Catholic kings were assassinated by Protestants, convinced of the righteousness and Godliness of their actions. Once killing legitimate rulers became fair game, there was no end to the possible violence. Any important personage who even considered negotiating a compromise settlement between warring religious groups, even if he had the sympathy of his subjects, left himself vulnerable to a brutal death. The spectre of regicide led many princes to rule over their subjects in an inquisitorial manner. Anyone disagreeing with royal religious policy was not merely a religious dissenter, but a traitor because every religiously subversive person was viewed as a possible assassin. A Catholic in Protestant England was often regarded as a religious deviant, who probably harbored dangerous foreign Jesuits. Similarly, a Protestant in a Catholic country was suspect because a truly loyal subject would not disagree with his ruler over religious policy, or so Catholic authorities argued. The effect was to undermine what few rights each subject possessed, and with each attempted assassination their number dwindled.

Terror tactics, assassination, and the reduction of the nonconforming individual to the status of possible traitor alienated many subjects from their prince; and because all this was perpetrated in the name of Christ, people grew increasingly wary of religious idealism. In time many of those who had been exposed to the suffering caused by rampant religious and political extremism came to doubt the truth of any religious persuasions.

In reaction to this state of affairs there gradually arose a cynical and skeptical approach to religion, God, and society. Its most eloquent spokesman was the renowned Church canon, Pierre Charron, who wrote: "The advice I give here to him who desires to be wise is to keep and observe in word and deed the laws and customs of the country where he lives, and that, not because of intrinsic justice or equity in these laws, but simply because they are the law and the custom . . . this is the mystical foundation of their authority, there is no other." According to Charron, it was no longer possible to accept the long held view that God was the basis of law and society, or even religion. One who is truly wise will simply follow the laws, and therefore embrace the religion of his state simply because that is the easiest way to stay out of trouble.

This approach to religion is often referred to as skeptical fideism, that is, belief and practice based on, and tempered by, skepticism. Charron and likeminded individuals separated the inward from the outward aspects of religion, preaching outward conformity to enable the individual to practice in the secret of his home whatever religion or irreligion he wished. While this was certainly good advice, considering the nature of the times of the late sixteenth century, it nevertheless points up the poor quality of the prevailing religious atmosphere. After decades of persecution and intolerance the only means of expression open to the individual was secret, shielded by a well cultivated apathy. Religion had lost any ability to influence the lives and morals of Europeans; and if God did exist, His spokesmen were obviously charlatans, to be tolerated and even feared.

One might well ask why religion in the sixteenth century was so divisive a social factor, and why the different religious persuasions would not compromise or arrange some sort of mutual toleration. In part the answer to this question lies in the nature of traditional Christianity itself. Because the sixteenth century placed such great emphasis on the importance of original sin and the depraved state in which man must find himself as a result of sinning, religion played a very significant role in society. It was only through religious belief and the church that man might redeem himself. If man did not redeem himself in this world, he would be damned to an eternity of hell in the world to come; and sixteenth century authors surpassed all others in depicting the horrors of hell.

Unfortunately, not all pious beliefs were thought to have redemptive powers. Consequently, the leaders of different religious denominations saw themselves providing man with a great service in persecuting holders of contrary views; for in so doing they were eliminating all "wrong" beliefs which would lead man to hell. The very idea of compromise had to be rejected since there could be no compromise with the devil or his agents on earth. It was not because of a lack of interdenominational negotiations that there was no religious peace in Europe. It was simply a matter of sheer obstinacy on the part of the churches themselves, which entered each series of conferences with the hope of converting the other side and, if need be, liquidating it.

IV

THE FRENCH CRISIS AND THE RESPONSE OF CATHERINE DE MEDICI

Perhaps the most disheartening consequence of extremism in sixteenth century religious thought was its deadly spillage and carryover into the political affairs of some of the major European states. Germany had to endure the bitterness and devastation of the Schmalkaldic wars. England suffered the agonies of the Henrician Reformation and the reigns of the Tudor Queens. The Netherlands were forced to experience nearly a century of repression and bloodletting.

Above all however, it was France that bore the curse of life's most sinister realities in the era of Reform and Counter-Reform, despite the fact that at the beginning of the sixteenth century this state had managed to attain the strength and prestige of the proudest Renaissance monarchy. During the reign of Francis I (1515-1547) the French crown could boast of an exceptionally rich endowment with natural resources as well as a significantly dense population, which easily paled into insignificance that of any of its rivals. Even more important were its vast financial resources, bolstered by the ever expandable tax revenues of the *taille*. In addition, the potentially troublesome Estates General met neither during the reign of Francis I nor of his successor Henry II (1547-1559), while the provincial estates caused their royal master little difficulty and were oftentimes successfully ignored or circumvented by him. Finally, in the year 1516 French royal power was massively increased by the enactment of the Concordat of Bologna. Negotiated in behalf of Francis I and Pope Leo X, it rescinded the Pragmatic Sanction of 1438 but placed the choice of all bishops and abbots squarely in the hands of His Most Christian Majesty. The practical effect of the Concordat of Bologna was to enable the French king—merely at the price of paying lip service to the spiritual and moral primacy of the Pope—to avail himself of the virtually limitless wealth of the Gallican Church. It is little wonder that on the eve of the Protestant Reformation the French monarchy was the envy of Europe, which fearfully observed the seemingly inexorable growth of its royal absolutism towards that ideal of ideals: *Une Foi, Un Roi, Une Loi.*

Yet, by the final quarter of the sixteenth century, France had fallen into a condition of chronic civil war in which extremist Catholics and Calvinists saw fit to propel their state to the threshold of destruction. The former, who gradually organized themselves into what became known as the "Holy League," looked to the Papacy and the Spanish King for inspiration as well as downright economic and military assistance. The latter, who emerged as the "Huguenot Party," frequently relied upon similar support from England, Geneva, Basle, and Protestant Germany. The main consequence of these developments was the reduction of France to an international battleground, helplessly victimized by centrifugal forces that threatened to blow it apart and facilitate an inevitable attempt by predatory neighbors to gobble it up. Indeed, during this time of troubles Philip II was quick to cast his greedy eyes upon Navarre and its bordering territories while Queen Elizabeth anxiously awaited an opportunity to recapture the French city of Calais. So desperate was the condition of France destined to become, that by 1588 even the

impecunious and habitually pusillanimous Duke of
Savoy would have the audacity to invade and seize a
portion of French territory.

How France managed to fall into such a pathetic
state, and how one very remarkable woman tirelessly
strove virtually to glue the realm together again constitute the subject matter of the present chapter.

* * * * *

The story of the near débacle of the French monarchy during the sixteenth century is primarily the story
of the Reformation in France, the beginning of which
dates from the year 1519, when the first wave of Lutheran books made their way across the eastern French
border. By 1540 the new religious movement had spread
into most rural areas with the possible exceptions of
only Auvergne and Brittany. Its most striking penetra-
tion, however, was in the cities of Paris and Meaux,
where Christian scholars and intellectuals had previously
been aroused by the conservative reforming tendencies
of Colet, Erasmus, and Lefèvre d'Étaples. As a matter of
fact, initially Lutheran sentiments were scarcely distin-
guishable from those expressed by contemporary Christian humanists of an Erasmian persuasion.

Soon enough however extremists emerged to throw
down the gauntlet to the Sorbonne, ridicule Catholic
theology, and of course denounce the Pope as the anti-
Christ. Lutheran provocation climaxed in the middle of
October 1534, when large placards inveighing against
and insulting the Mass were set up at several strategic
locations in Paris, Orleans, Rouen, Blois, Tours, (and
even on the very doors to the King's bedroom at
Amboise). At this point the die was clearly cast. Protestantism had taken hold in France.

Yet, in order for the Reformation to retain a firm
grip upon its new Gallic votaries, it would eventually
have to consititue far more than merely a loosely organ-

ized German importation with homogeneously lackluster leadership. Dissatisfied French Christians required
a dynamic, charismatic, (and above all) native religious
c r u s a d e r , who would preside over a non-
establishmentarian faith graced with far more revolutionary fervor and zeal than any brand of transplanted,
mid-sixteenth century Lutheranism could possibly mus-
ter. Soon enough however, their needs were more than
satisfied by the emergence of John Calvin, whose stark,
forbidding figure would virtually dominate the Reformation movement during its most formative years.

Issuing directives from the city of Geneva (which he
literally ruled for twenty-four years), Calvin gave French
Protestants astoundingly effective leadership, a remark-
ably co-ordinated and synthesized theological system,
and a rigidly disciplined Church organization, which has
quite adequately been described as a new Catholicism
outside the old and fanatically opposed to it. As the
reign of King Henry II reached its abrupt end, the new,
animated, militant Huguenot faith, (by which name
French Calvinism gradually became known) was already
burgeoning with such large numbers of fervent prose-
lytes as to enable it to pose a serious threat to the
spiritual predominance that had traditionally been enjoyed—and abused—by the Gallican Church.

The reasons for the widespread and enthusiastic response to this hyper-Augustinian heresy were legion.
French Catholicism could not or would not face up to
the challenge of Erasmus and likeminded individuals by
putting its house in order. Instead it chose to continue
wallowing in its deplorable condition characterized by
corruption, concubinage, and ignorance. In the province
of Brittany during the early sixteenth century clerical
absenteeism had become so endemic that not one parish
in fifty could boast of its pastor being in residence.
Lorraine was "graced" with a cardinal (appointed at age
twenty-three), who possessed a royally bestowed *carte*

blanche to gobble up the revenues of three bishoprics and no less than eleven extremely lucrative abbeys. One contemporary witness mournfully reported that most French priests were virtually submerged in a miasma of penury and ignorance—ninety per cent of them being totally unable to read their own language, let alone that of their Church. In general the spiritual needs of the French people were as shamefully ignored as the misery and privation they were forced to endure because of galloping inflation, crushing taxation, and an endless series of wars presided over by His Most Christian Majesty.

It is no wonder that during the 1540's and 1550's large numbers of unemployed, despairing workers, artisans, and shopkeepers readily embraced the new faith that was so staunchly opposed to the predatory, insensitive, scandal-ridden Catholic establishment. They were quickly joined by university students and faculty, itinerant friars, physicians, lawyers, and merchants. Then came droves of petty nobles, whose fixed incomes could no longer support them in an era of constantly rising prices. Finally, on the eve of the Peace of Cateau-Cambrésis the Huguenot movement became infused with the power and prestige of a number of France's political heavyweights: aristocratic grandees and even princes of the blood. Among this illustrious group were found Antoine de Bourbon, the King of Navarre; his irresponsible, pugnacious brother, the Prince de Condé; Admiral Gaspard de Coligny, perhaps the most capable soldier in the entire realm; and his brother, Francois d'Andelot.

By mid 1559 well over two thousand separate Huguenot Churches were functioning in France, all of them tightly organized into a strict, exceedingly manageable hierarchical structure. At the base of the ecclesiastical pyramid were the local churches, each governed by a Consistory (composed of the minister and lay elders).

Individual churches were grouped into districts, which
in turn were supervised by assemblies called Colloquies.
The latter owed obedience to the provincial Synods,
which were finally responsible to the National synod,
consisting of two ministers and two elders recruited
from every province in France.

With the conversion of large elements of the French
nobility to Calvinism there rapidly grew within the
Huguenot movement a military organization which be-
came superimposed upon its ecclesiastical pyramid.
Soon every Huguenot church was under the protection
of a noble, referring to himself as its captain, every
Colloquy under the protection of its "colonel," every
Provincial Synod, its *chef général.*

This mingling of institutionalized, religious fanaticism
with irresponsible, aristocratic instigation inevitably
placed the French monarchy squarely on the top of a
political powder keg. With the death of King Henry II
its long fuse began to burn.

* * * * *

Once Reformation ideas had made their initial, tortu-
ous infiltration into France, the forces of Catholic ob-
scurantism were quick to react. Spearheaded by such
bastions of religious orthodoxy as the Sorbonne and the
Parlement of Paris, a thoroughly intransigent, anti-
Protestant offensive unleashed its fury against all proponents of theological modification, whether they be
sympathetic to Luther or merely to the Catholic
Lefèvre.

By the summer of 1526 even the mildest criticism of
Catholic authorities was viewed as tantamount to the
commission of an act of heresy, punishable by imprisonment or worse. Three years earlier Louis de Berquin,
whose "crime" was to have translated Erasmus, suddenly found himself cast into the Conciergerie and condemned to death. His life was spared only through the

direct intervention of no less a figure than the King of France himself. Others were not so fortunate. With the capture of Francis I by Spanish troops in 1525 at the Battle of Pavia came the worst wave of repression thus far, as hyperzealous Catholics, led by Noel Béda of the Sorbonne hierarchy, rapidly came to believe that they possessed a *carte blanche* to seek out and destroy all deviations from the Church Universal. A full-fledged reign of terror was averted only by the return to France of its King, who arriving back in late 1526 had to forcefully inform his exuberant courtiers that their domestic heretic-baiting could easily succeed in demolishing the best efforts of his tenuous foreign policy, which desperately required good relations between himself and the more important European Protestant rulers. Moreover, it demanded little imagination on the part of the wily French monarch to perceive the utter futility of any attempt by his state to bring the despised Holy Roman Emperor to heel, if it were to remain a house divided against itself.

In his attempt to at least minimize the persecution of French Protestants Francis was encouraged and assisted by a heterogeneous group of humanist intellectuals, who as one scholar has put it: " . . .aimed at bringing men together and at keeping them within traditional Christianity by charity rather than force, by moral reforms rather than by dogmatic discussion, by a return to the Bible and the Fathers rather than by the idle subtleties of a decadent Scholasticism." This devoted group, which even managed to convince the King to invite the renowned Lutheran theologian, Philipp Melanchthon, to visit Paris and debate with the Faculty of Theology, was completely dedicated to effecting any and all reforms in the Church that could enhance its purity without destroying its unity.

Yet in the last analysis both humanists and King failed in their policy of reconciliation. The former could never generate the endorsement of more than a tiny minority of their countrymen, while their intellectual adversaries in the Sorbonne and the Parlement of Paris enjoyed the overwhelming support of ordinary French folk, saturated as they were with bigotry and ignorance. Moreover, it could hardly be said that the humanist movement was seconded by the majority of French Protestants, who instead, gradually becoming dominated by the militant doctrines of John Calvin, unequivocally rejected all offers of religious compromise. As for Francis I, by the summer of 1538 his policy of alliance with Protestant powers had collapsed. Consequently, in the ensuing years he would have little inclination to circumvent the party of persecution, now led by the Constable de Montmorency, whose orthodoxy was as uncompromising as his lifelong loyalty to the French crown.

Almost inevitably, the remaining years of Francis I's reign were stigmatized by royal condonation of an albeit spasmodic but nevertheless inexcusably savage and mindless Protestant pogrom. On the eve of his death Francis was jarred from his apathy with the news that over a thousand non-Catholics from Provence had been recently slaughtered. Unfortunately, at this late date expressions of kingly sorrow meant and accounted for little in a realm that would during the next reign be even less inclined to express the quality of mercy, however strained.

* * * * *

Francis I had been for the major part of his reign an innovative, charmingly humorous, charismatic leader who usually managed to restrain himself from formulating inflexible royal policies, despite the intensity of his personal feelings. However, his lackluster and least favored son, who succeeded him as Henry II, was sadly wanting of Francis' good qualities, being instead a sullen, dyspeptic, utterly unimaginative bigot.

One of Henry's first official acts provided for the creation in Parlement of a special chamber, called the *Chambre ardente*, that was entrusted to try heretics of all types. In just over two years of operation this new tribunal handled some five hundred cases with brutal efficiency. In 1551 the heretic-hunting sovereign issued the Edict of Chateaubriand, which stipulated that one-third of the belongings of a convicted Protestant might be turned over by the royal government to anyone who was instrumental in bringing such an individual to "justice." Furthermore, upon the suggestion of the Papal legate, the redoubtable Cardinal Caraffa, Henry II even toyed with the idea of introducing the Roman Inquisition into his own realm. Only the opposition of Gallican ideologists precluded this, and instead induced him to settle for the enactment of a law which would endow the cardinals of Lorraine, Bourbon, and Châtillon with inquisitorial powers. Six years later the King issued the Edict of Compiègne, which prescribed the death penalty for all convicted heretics.

Yet the Protestant movement in France continued to grow, partially because its adherents, like the early Christians, throve in the face of persecution, and partially because Henry's foreign entanglements consumed too much of his energy and resources to enable him to deal effectively with even the most pressing domestic affairs. When in May of 1558 intervention by a number of German princes in favor of his Protestant subjects threw his frustrations into high relief, His Most Christian Majesty is said to have thundered: "I swear that if I can settle my foreign affairs, I shall make the blood and the heads of that infamous Lutheran rabble run through the streets."

In April of the next year the Treaty of Cateau-Cambrésis finally put France at peace with her foreign adversaries and allowed Henry II to pursue in earnest his

holy war against all nonconforming subjects. Two
months later he issued the Edict of Écouen, providing
for the systematic extirpation of heresy by means of
expulsion, imprisonment, and execution.

This meant war to the knife; and French Protestants,
who by this date were mainly Calvinists (Huguenots),
answered the challenge with an unprecedented tenacity
and the grimest determination. They immediately seized
control of towns, especially in the southern and western
portions of the realm, where they looted Catholic
Churches, brutalized priests, raped nuns, exacted trib-
ute, and eventually raised a regular army to help them
construct their own *de facto* state inside of France.

* * * * *

On 10 July 1559 Henry II died suddenly and unex-
pectedly, which meant that from this day to the final
decade of the sixteenth century the destiny of France
would be technically in the hands of three of his sons:
Francis II (1559-62), Charles IX (1562-74), and Henry
III (1574-89). The first, virtually a physical wreck,
would breathe his last before reaching the age of eighteen; the second, dullwitted and paranoid, would fall
constant prey to the most sinister forces at court; the
third and perhaps most capable proved to be too frivo-
lous and dissolute to endear himself to his subjects.
Were it simply up to these men, France would have
shortly been torn to shreds by the warring factions of
the hyper-Catholic "Holy League" and the equally
fanatical Huguenot Party. Both possessed the requisite
strength to knock the French crown off the dizzy head
of its royal master. The fact that this never took place
was due only to the relentless exertions of the Queen-
Mother, Catherine de Medici, a woman with a will of
iron, an intellect well above the average, and a dogged
determination to look after the best interests of her sons
and their elusive kingdom.

Soon after his accession to the throne Francis II fell under the sway of the "Holy League," at the head of which stood Francis, Duke of Guise, and his brother the Cardinal of Lorraine. Moreover, the powerful influence, exerted by this organization, on the new king was rapidly enhanced by the latter's own wife, the renowned Mary Queen of Scots, who happened to be a niece of the Guise patriarchs. These ardent Catholics successfully conspired to convince His Most Christian Majesty to renew the savage persecutions of his father's reign.

Huguenot reaction consequently assumed the form of an armed rebellion, motivated by the political ambitions of the Bourbon family as well as genuinely religious fervor. Encouraged by the Prince de Condé, and fortified with English subsidies, a band of insurrectionists planned to organize themselves near Amboise, where the royal court was in residence (March 1560), kidnap the king (supposedly for his own protection against the designs of the Guise family), and forcefully help induce a new royal policy towards those Frenchmen who had embraced the Calvinist faith. Unfortunately for the Bourbons, this movement was nipped in the bud.

Thoroughly outraged, Francis II ordered the Duke of Guise to seek out and destroy any and all conspirators—a task which the commander of the "Holy League" was only too happy to perform. Immediately, a flock of not so eminent Huguenot heads began to roll. Condé of course managed to escape royal vengeance by relying upon his high birth with its attendant privileges, and categorically denying any complicity in the seditious movement. His captain, La Renaudie, assigned the dubious honor of having instigated the plot, was not so fortunate.

With the Conspiracy of Amboise the French Wars of Religion had begun; and they in all probability would have continued unabated if it were not for the intervention at this juncture of the Queen-Mother, who was determined to assume *de facto* royal power in order to protect the crucial interests of France against the centrifugal forces of both the Huguenot Party and the "Holy League." Having nervously gazed upon the bitter fruit of unbridled religious fanaticism, she convinced herself that only an official royal policy of conciliation could succeed in preventing the state from self-destructing.

Catherine knew full well that were it not for the assistance that her son, dominated by his wife and her Guise uncles, had been rendering to the Scottish crown, Elizabeth would have declined Condé's request for subsidization. Therefore, in order to prevent further English meddling in internal French affairs, the Queen-Mother abruptly informed Mary Queen of Scots to look outside of France for all future support in her struggles against the English state.

Even more important, through the Edict of Amboise (2 March 1560) Catherine induced her son to nullify the intransigent Edict of Écouen, which had virtually amounted to a declaration of war by the previous king against all his non-Catholic subjects. A few weeks later the Huguenots were given the right to petition Francis II to redress their outstanding grievances, while provision also was made to summon a national council that would examine, discuss, and hopefully resolve all religious problems in France. Finally, an amnesty was granted to nonviolent, lay religious offenders; and all secular authorities were forbidden to try any individuals for heresy.

For her commendable efforts, the Queen-Mother was dubbed "that meddling Florentine merchant" by the Holy League and "that whore who is infecting us with her leprosy" by the Huguenot Party. Nevertheless, she persisted with her policies of conciliation. In May of 1560 Catherine appointed to the chancellorship, Michel de l'Hospital, a reputed jurist and financier, who was determined to impose upon France some sort of religious peace. If this could be achieved under the auspices of an all-embracing Christian humanism, de l'Hospital would have been more than pleased. However, failing this, the chancellor was not above considering pure political expedience as the major tool in the construction of and justification for a viable alternative to incessant civil strife.

The conciliatory policies of de l'Hospital and his patroness were given considerable momentum by the Council of Fontainebleau, which met during the month of August 1560 in a spirit of measured ecumenicity. Its proceedings were climaxed with a declaration by Francis II, in which he vowed to call the Estates General as well as a national council and to end all religious litigations, except those which had to be carried out against "fools."

By the middle of December the Estates General was ready to convene in the city of Orleans. It would however do so under a new king, a nine year old boy, who became Charles IX with the tragic death of his brother on 5 December. The former would be thoroughly dominated by his mother, who managed to seize the regency thanks in great measure to another of the never ending series of *faux pas* committed by the rambunctious Prince de Condé.

This hot-headed Bourbon had recently gambled on a new conspiracy, that was quickly aborted by the annihilation of his army, after which he was thrown into jail. While Condé awaited trial on a charge of high treason, Francis II breathed his last, allowing the would-be traitor's brother, Antoine de Bourbon, to assert his constitutional prerogative of acting as regent for the new king. At this point, summoning all her Machiavellian talents, Catherine both bribed and intimidated the spineless King of Navarre into renouncing his claim. In return for this favor, she dropped all charges against his brother, promised to let bygones be bygones, and granted him a prestigious but politically vacuous title.

This maneuver constituted a veritable *tour de force* by the Queen-Mother, who was now unquestionably the power behind the throne, having not merely succeeded in becoming regent but also having managed to neutralize simultaneously the strength of both the Bourbon and Guise factions. The former clearly lost their chance to occupy a pivotal position in the new royal government. The latter failed to retain the grip they had held on the previous monarch and were forced to witness the unceremonious banishment of their illustrious relative, Mary Queen of Scots, from the realm of her dead husband.

It was on this note of ascendancy for the political center that the Estates General made their deliberations. The sessions were highlighted by the rhetoric of Michel de l'Hospital which focused on the threats that religious fanaticism on both sides could present to the very life of the French state. In his initial address the chancellor admonished: "The knife can do little against the spirit, apart from destroying the soul as well as the body. . . . Christians argue in vain that they take up arms for God's cause, because God's cause does not require an armed defense. Our religion was neither started nor maintained nor preserved by force of arms."

In the last analysis de l'Hospital argued, as did the Queen-Mother, that domestic tranquility could only be achieved by the calling of a national council, which just might be able to repair the badly cracked edifice of Christianity. Such a body was brought into existence in September 1561.

Certain preparations however had to be made for its initiation. In the first place, some degree of freedom of conscience had to be at least provisionally established in France. To this end the royal edict of 19 April was promulgated. It commanded the Holy League and the

Huguenot Party to cease hurling insults at one another; prohibited forced entries into private homes for the purpose of discovering and incarcerating conventiclers; ordered the release of all prisoners who had been jailed for religious reasons; and guaranteed recalcitrant Protestants the right of free exit from France after having an opportunity to sell their lands.

More important was the need to obfuscate papal scrutiny of what His Holiness could only regard as a dangerous challenge by the renegade Gallican Church to Roman supremacy within the fold of Catholicism. When such an attempt to mesmerize the Pope aborted, causing him to reopen the Council of Trent in order to invalidate the French national council completely, Catherine countered by blithely substituting the name "colloquy" for council, and then proceeding without the slightest modification in plans.

When the Colloquy of Poissy, as it was called, began its sessions, in attendance were such notorious heretics as Peter Martyr and Theodore Beza, both protected by royal safe-conducts. Catherine, who had little sensitivity or appreciation for dogmatics and apologetics, simplistically hoped that these Protestant theologians would sit down and calmly "talk sense" with their Catholic counterparts until an amicable resolution to all outstanding problems could be achieved.

The results of this dialogue were of course predictable. De l'Hospital was scorned; Catherine was ridiculed; and the policy of reconciliation suffered a severe reverse. When all negotiations entirely broke down, the Catholic theologians intransigently reaffirmed the cardinal doctrine of transubstantiation, anathematizing anyone who might dare to believe differently.

Moreover, the presence of Protestant leaders in France for the meetings at Poissy gave heart to some obstreperous elements in the Huguenot rank and file, who saw this as an occasion to seize and plunder Cath-

olic Churches. The Catholics in turn reacted by massa-
cring Huguenots all over the map of France. Finally,
three of the foremost Catholic nobles: the Duke de
Guise, the Constable de Montmorency, and the Marshal
de Saint-André, viewing with alarm the growth of
Huguenot power and prestige, settled their own differences and formed a triumvirate dedicated to defending
the Catholic Faith in collaboration with, or if need be
even in spite of, the French King himself.

As far as the Queen-Mother and her chancellor were
concerned, the miserable failure of the Colloquy of
Poissy proved that there were now but two ways in
which to solve the denominational conflict that continued to plague France with increasing intensity: a
wholesale renewal of Henry II's persecution tactics or
the establishment of a revolutionary royal policy, based
on complete civil toleration of the Huguenots, in the
hope that national unity might thus be achieved, albeit
at the expense of the absolutist dream: *Une Foi, Un
Roi, Une Loi*. Quickly discarding the first alternative,
mainly because of its proven unworkability, Catherine
decided to make her appeal to the growing number of
moderates in both religious camps. In this new policy
she received not only the predictable support of de
l'Hospital, but also that of a dedicated body of political
theorists, who thought of themselves as "good Frenchmen" more readily than as religious sectarians, and who
would subsequently organize themselves into what became known as the *Politique* Party.

Acting immediately upon the advice of his mother,
Charles IX promulgated the Edict of January 1562,
which gave official recognition to the Protestant
churches in France. Non-Catholic religious services were
condoned in all areas except those which contained such
a preponderance of die-hard Catholics that a serious
threat would be posed to the safety of minority wor-
shipers.

Although the Pope actually allowed himself to be
convinced that the Edict of January was necessary to
avoid even greater concessions to Huguenot malcon-
tents, an exceedingly dim view of Catherine's new policy was taken by the Holy League, one member of
which passionately advocated the casting of this troublesome shrew into the Seine River. Fortified by the
treacherous abandonment of the Protestant cause by
Antoine de Bourbon, the Catholic triumvirate actively
planned to take up arms against the Queen-Mother "in
the name of the King." When Catherine subsequently
appealed to Condé for help the latter gave his consent,
but only because he felt there was something to be
gained by supporting the enemies of the triumvirate.

The inevitable outbreak of hostilities followed an unfortunate incident which took place on 1 March in the
town of Vassy, where the Duke de Guise, accompanied
by some soldiers, had just happened to stop in order to
hear Mass. The Church that Guise planned to attend was
located close to a barn where a group of the local
Huguenots had gathered, contrary to the terms of the
Edict of January. A quarrel, which quickly developed
between them and the Duke's retainers, ended in a
massacre by the latter of about sixty men and women.

Although Catherine and Beza, (who had not yet de-
parted from the French court), urged that the horrible
affair be settled by legal means, violence could not be
prevented. Almost immediately the commanders of
both armies lost control of their troops, who committed
the most brutal atrocities whenever it suited them to do
so.

In the long run however the war had to be considered
as a major victory for the Queen-Mother since it brought
about the deaths of three chronic trouble-makers:
Antoine de Bourbon, the Marshal de Sainte-André, and
the Duke de Guise himself, who was assassinated with
the probable connivance of Admiral de Coligny. More-

over, the Constable de Montmorency and the Prince de
Condé were captured during the hostilities.

The peace, which was established by the Edict of
Amboise in March 1563, promised to be reasonably dur-
able, (and did indeed prevent further warfare for four
years). Furthermore, in the negotiations Condé thought
only of securing religious liberties for the upper crust of
French society, all of which had the effect of leading
common folk to believe that Protestantism had become
the religion of the aristocracy. Therefore, as long as
Condé remained among the living, Catherine would not
have to contend with the prospect of a new wave of
mass conversions to the rebel faith.

During the years immediately following the Edict of
Amboise, when small religious disturbances threatened
to shatter France's relative domestic tranquility, the
Queen-Mother conspired to nip them in the bud through
the strategic use of what became known as her "Flying
Squadron." This organization consisted of approximately twenty of the most alluring, curvacious, readily
corruptible females, specially trained by Catherine to
exploit their manifest charms in such a way as to induce
both Catholic and Huguenot warlords to spend as much
time as possible out of their saddles and off their feet. It
was hoped that once the potential peace-wreckers fell
victims to the *douce violence* of the "Flying Squadron,"
they would become so involved with sweet nonsense as
to incapacitate themselves for further exertions such as
the perpetuating of civil war in France.

Unfortunately however, neither the Edict of Amboise
nor Catherine's highly skilled, well endowed staff could
prevent war forever; and by the autumn of 1567 the
religious factions in France were once again at each
other's throats. The occasion for this new outbreak of
violence was the invasion of the Spanish Netherlands by
the nefarious Duke of Alva, one of Philip II's most vi-
cious and fanatical generals.

Initially the Huguenots marked time until they could
determine Catherine's reaction to this alarming growth
of Spanish power in a neighboring state. And for her
part the Queen-Mother was so displeased with the
Duke's activities that she even refused him permission to
march his troops through French territory in order to
gain a tactical advantage over the rebellious Dutch Protestants. Unfortunately, the Huguenots did not hear of
this rebuff, realizing only that Catherine had recently
traveled to Bayonne to talk with her daughter Elizabeth
(who happened to be the Queen of Spain) about matters
which were not disclosed.

Finally when news reached France that Alva had
treacherously arrested two highly popular Dutch
leaders, Egmont and Horn, the Huguenot Party jumped
to the conclusion that the Queen-Mother was planning a
similar fate for them. Therefore, they decided to beat
her to the punch. On 30 September, the day after the
feast of St. Michael, a band of French Calvinists attacked the residence of the Bishop of Nîmes, killing
eighty priests, nuns, and laymen. Five days before this
massacre, which became known as the *Michelade*, the
tempestuous Condé had made yet another abortive attempt to kidnap Charles IX and his mother, this time
near the city of Meaux. Smarting from his failure, he
shortly thereafter laid siege to Paris with his troops.

Catherine was thoroughly outraged, and in the ensuing war lent substantial support to the Catholic
armies. Shortly after the outbreak of hostilities, the
Queen-Mother lucidly expressed her enmity towards the
duplicitous Huguenots in a communication to the lieu-
tenant-general of the Dauphiné, in which she exclaimed:
" . . . cut to pieces, without sparing a single one, all who
give active support to those [Huguenots] because the
more that die, the fewer enemies there are."

Her behavior in this instance has been criticized by
many historians as illustrative of her alleged incompe-

tence to deal effectively with crucial affairs of state.
These detractors have portrayed Catherine as a paro-
chial, hyper-possessive meddler in matters which far ex-
ceeded her powers of comprehension—a mother hen
who would not tolerate even the mildest incursion into
the sphere of influence she had set up around the
French throne. It has been further maintained that
those who dared to challenge the control she exercised
over her offspring suffered nothing short of the most
dreadful consequences.

Yet in all fairness to the Queen-Mother, it has to be
admitted that she was betrayed far more than she de-
served to be by the rather sinister Huguenot leadership.
For the past seventeen years she had literally racked her
brain for a functional compromise that might possibly
put an end to the endemic feuding in the realm of her
sons. She had appealed to Christian Humanists, *politiques*, and the Pope himself as well as to the leaders of
the Holy League and the Huguenot Party to endorse her
politics of conciliation. The results of her whirlwind activity were demoralizing, to say the least. She learned
the depressing lessons of all great compromisers from
Solon to Castellio, namely that the fruit of their agoniz-
ing labors rarely if ever satisfies anyone for an appreciable period of time.

In any case, the war that had been started by the
Michelade was mercifully brief, consisting of little more
than the battle of Saint-Denis, in which the aging Constable de Montmorency finally met his end. In March
1568 all parties signed the Peace of Longjumeau, which
essentially parroted the terms of the Edict of Amboise.

Regrettably however, even after the treaty was made
official, hostilities continued generally unabated in not
only France but also the Netherlands, where their bitterness increased after the execution of Egmont and Horn
by the Duke of Alva. By autumn of the same year, war
was again literally declared between French Catholics

and Huguenots. At this point the beleaguered chancellor, Michel de l'Hospital, suddenly went into retirement. Belittlers of the Queen-Mother oftentimes accuse her of having discharged and disgraced her hard-working fellow traveler in a fit of anger. Actually, it is not at all clear what role Catherine played in his retirement; and in all probability it was de l'Hospital himself who took the initiative, feeling that a resurrection of the policies of Henry II was now inevitable and desiring not to witness it in any official capacity. Eleven days after the new war began, he turned in his seals to the King.

Once again the Queen-Mother felt perniciously betrayed by the Huguenots, who it seemed had plotted a resumption of hostilities before the ink had dried on the Treaty of Longjumeau. So intense did her rancor become that she even conspired to seize and possibly execute Condé and Coligny. The plan misfired however as its intended victims were warned in time to flee from the French capital. Once safely behind the walls of La Rochelle, the Huguenot leaders quickly prepared themselves for what would become their most ferocious encounter with the Catholic enemy.

The war, which followed immediately, consisted of an incredible succession of atrocities committed by both sides with unrelenting savagery. The Huguenots murdered, pillaged, raped, burned, and fanatically slaughtered women and children. They were especially cruel to Catholic priests, in one instance taking a monastery and forcing the monks to hang one another.

The Catholics behaved even worse, if that is possible. Several of their grisly mobs boasted of having tossed Huguenot infants into the air in order to impale them with pikes. Others made a sport of dragging denuded Huguenots through the streets of France and shortly thereafter drowning them in sewers. Catholic soldiers threw helpless victims into ovens, hacked them to pieces, and skinned them alive. After Condé lost the

Battle of Jarnac and was forced to surrender to a Catholic army, one of its members casually shot him in the back.

In August 1570 peace came once again to a state that had never before experienced such horrifying and brutal anarchy. In two years of warfare France had become bankrupt, while the gutters of virtually all its cities ran with the blood of innocent people. Now France was ready for one more compromise, the Edict of Saint-Germain, the terms of which would be hammered out by the leading *politiques*, to be endorsed by the Queen-Mother, who had reconvinced herself that the problems of the realm could only be solved through moderation.

Such a maneuver was bound to enrage the Guise faction, which had quite understandably been enjoying an ascendancy at court during the war years. Catherine however not only reconciled herself to the potentialities of her "exacerbating" tactics; she viewed them with a measure of vicarious satisfaction, as the pompous Catholic nobility and their ubiquitous Spanish side-kicks had during their brief period of dominance quite characteristically managed to make themselves totally obnoxious to both her family and herself.

The Edict of Saint-Germain, a far less restrictive document than those which were drawn up to help terminate the preceding two wars, provided for a general amnesty; allowed Huguenots to worship freely in the suburbs of two towns per province as well as have access to schools, universities, and hospitals; and finally turned over to these religious rebels, for their utilization during the next two years, four sanctuaries—La Rochelle, Montauban, Cognac, and La Charité.

To reinforce the era of good feelings that she hoped to create between moderate Catholics and their Protestant counterparts, the Queen-Mother offered the hand in marriage of her daughter, Marguerite de Valois, to Henry Bourbon, the new king of Navarre and titular leader of the Huguenot Party. In addition, she proposed that her second son, the Duke d'Anjou, become the husband of Elizabeth of England; and although the latter never fulfilled Catherine's fondest expectations, this did not deter the "Good Queen Bess" from negotiating a much-desired defensive alliance with France directed against Spanish territorial ambitions.

However not even this impressive spate of conciliatory diplomacy could prevent hapless France from suffering the agonies of yet another blood bath, the causes of which would come from a war that had recently broken out between Spain and the Netherlands. In April 1572 the capture of the strategic city of Brille by the Dutch Sea Beggars appeared to present some of the *politiques*, (who were seconded by the Huguenot Party), with a ready-made scheme that, if executed properly, would enable all patriotic Frenchmen to forget their domestic animosities and join together in a crusade against a common foe. This goal, amounting to a sixteenth century *union sacré*, could be achieved, it was argued, through joining the Dutch rebels in an all-out effort to seriously cripple the military capacity of Spain, which would incidentally produce the added effect of allowing France to break out of the deadly vice of Habsburg encirclement.

As appealing as a new war with Spain seemed at first glance, little thought on Catherine's part was required to convince her of the folly of such an undertaking. It was to proceed at a time when France had already been terribly weakened by its long years of internecine feuding and when this tortured state could moreover expect little real help from England, which quite clearly in the final analysis wished a plague on both Habsburgs and Valois. Especially upsetting to the Queen-Mother was the manner in which Admiral de Coligny had captured the favor and enthusiasm of her son, who she was convinced would be exploited to the hilt by this unprincipled Huguenot chieftain in his plan to squander away France's remaining resources to achieve an impossible dream. The climax came when on 6 August 1572 Coligny arrogantly threatened Catherine with a new civil war if she refused to proceed wholeheartedly with the Spanish expedition.

Once again the Queen-Mother had been betrayed by the Huguenots, this time in the very midst of her most conscientious attempts to offer them a viable manner in which to coexist with their religious rivals. In her mind, which was not unfamiliar with the political teachings of a fellow Italian, Niccolò Machiavelli, there seemed to remain but one way of dealing with the desperate situation in which France now found itself: the assassination of Admiral de Coligny.

It took Catherine little time to lay the groundwork for this deed, since the opportunity for its performance as well as the requisite manpower were already at hand. By the middle of August all the great nobles of the realm, Coligny included, had taken up temporary residence in Paris to attend the wedding of Henry Bourbon and Marguerite de Valois, which took place on the eighteenth of the month. And, according to plan, four days later a faceless agent of the Duke de Guise, (the latter having never forgiven Coligny for his apparent complicity in the murder of the previous Duke), attempted (but failed) to cut the Admiral down with a harquebus, managing only to inflict an arm wound. Immediately, the Huguenots vowed to avenge their hero, with or without royal approval.

This unexpected turn of events clearly placed the Queen-Mother in an exceedingly dangerous situation, because although the Guise faction eagerly prepared to defend themselves, there was no guarantee that they would do so without openly acknowledging her involvement in their abortive plot. Therefore, fearing for her own life as well as the inevitable resumption of civil war,

Catherine decided once again to conspire with the Guises, this time to inflict a knockout blow on the Huguenot Party by murdering all its leaders, who were still residing in the French capital.

After browbeating the malleable King into condoning this diabolical scheme, Catherine and her accomplices quickly drew up a battle plan scheduling the slaughter for the early hours of St. Bartholemew's Day, 24 August 1572. Coligny, the first to die, was followed directly by every other prominent Huguenot with the exception of Henry Bourbon and the new Prince de Condé, who were allowed to convert to Catholicism on the spot; and Montgomery and Ferrières, who managed to escape the carnage. As soon as the predominantly Roman Catholic population of Paris realized what was happening, it exuberantly indulged itself in an orgy of bestiality that gave quarter to neither women nor innocent children. Finally, the sport was taken up in the Catholic provinces; and before it ended, approximately 20,000 people were dead.

European reaction to the St. Bartholemew's Day Massacre of course varied, with Protestant states looking upon it with shock and disgust while the Catholic powers joyfully received the news of its achievements. A typically Protestant response was that of the "Good Queen Bess," who—blithely dismissing her own systematic and sometimes savage persecution of English Catholics—melodramatically received the French ambassador in mourning clothes.

On the other side of the coin, Pope Gregory XIII ordered that the actions of 24 August be celebrated by a singing of the *Te Deum* in the basilica of St. Mark. Moreover, after publicly comparing Catherine de Medici to the Biblical Judith and Admiral de Coligny to Holofernes, the Pontiff had a medal struck in honor of the momentous event.

The manner in which His Holiness justified the indis-

criminate slaughter is reminiscent of the rationalizations
submitted by key American officials some three hundred seventy years later in defense of the atomic bomb-
ing of selected Japanese cities. Gregory XIII argued:
"For a number of years both sides had been brutally
struggling with each other . . . many lives being lost. Was
it not more economical and even more humane to finish
[the war] once and for all, particularly if this saved
Catholic lives?"

* * * * *

Perhaps the greatest tragedy of the St. Bartholemew's
Day Massacre comes from the fact that in one single
blow the entire work of setting up a viable system of
civil tolerance in France, on which Catherine de Medici
had so diligently labored for twelve painful, frustrating
years, seemed to be reduced to an exercise in utter futility. The Queen-Mother would never live to see halcyon
times in the realm of her sons.

In any event, much has been written in scathing criticism of Catherine's role in the disaster of 24 August as
well as her general policies. With regard to the former, it
has been argued that the St. Bartholemew's Day Massacre was as senseless as it was abominable. Not only is it
thoroughly impossible to justify such calculated, appall-
ing butchery; but Machiavelli himself would have
scorned the tactics of the Queen-Mother since, if anything, they actually strengthened the Huguenot Party,
the members of which soon began to enjoy the kind of
fervent, infectious support that is traditionally lavished
only upon martyrs.

As for Catherine's general policies, it has been alleged
that they invariably amounted to nothing more than a
hodgepodge of simpleminded solutions to extremely
complex problems, the very nature of which were un-
fathomable to this misguided woman, who consistently
confused her mastery in the art of intrigue with a

genuine ability to comprehend and come to grips effectively with the principles of European statecraft. Critics and detractors have repeatedly accused her of being little more than a predatory Italian adventuress, bereft of any real compassion for the agony of France and thoroughly incapable of grasping the deep-rooted emotions involved in the Religious Wars that she pretentiously sought to terminate.

In her defense however it should be pointed out that the St. Bartholemew's Day Massacre may be viewed as a highly logical application of French reason of state, which most contemporary political theorists would have condemned merely on the grounds that it was only "half done." Moreover, one ought not to lose sight of the crucial fact that for the overwhelming majority of mid-sixteenth century Frenchmen, toleration of the Huguenots was virtually incomprehensible, as they were assumed to be guilty not only of heresy, but also of murder, pillage, rape, and treason. As one author has stated: "When the royal government seemed to put an end to that continuous surrendering, [which is what French Catholics felt the various edicts of pacification amounted to] albeit in the most brutal way, everything seemed permissible in order to square accounts with the Reformation and to destroy it once and for all."

Finally, a balanced evaluation of Catherine's importance in the confrontation and conciliation that characterized Reformation France is quite impossible unless it is realized that in her attempts to bring peace to a troubled and perplexed land—for whatever reasons—she was enthusiastically supported by the most forward looking Catholic humanists as well as highly astute, clear thinking *politiques*. It was the policies of the latter group, borrowed in great part from Catherine's vast storehouse of political and religious compromises, that eventually formed the basis of the final solution to the anarchy of the Wars of Religion under the auspices of perhaps the greatest of all post-Medieval French monarchs, Henry IV.

It is undeniable that the mother of the last Valois kings possessed character deficiencies of major significance. Yet the fact remains that for twelve arduous years, with exceptional adroitness and fortitude, she managed to initiate a program of legal tolerance in France which averted far more catastrophes than it created. Had this remarkable woman not been cursed with a government that was simply too weak to cope effectively with its chronic civil wars, despite every sacrifice she selflessly made to achieve the elusive goal of domestic tranquility, history would have been far kinder to Catherine de Medici.

* * * * *

V

THE ENGLISH CRISIS
AND ITS RESOLUTION

The initiator of the English Reformation possessed a character, that embodied few of the virtues which helped define the aspirations and innovations of his continental counterparts. Henry VIII lacked the profundity, conviction, and self-discipline of the soul-searching Luther. Unlike Zwingli and, for that matter, most of his humanist contemporaries, he seemed incapable of expressing any deep-rooted sensitivity and compassion for his fellow man. The acumen, religious fervor, and unimpeachable morality of John Calvin were totally foreign to him.

Even his apologists, whether they be sixteenth century court-sycophants or modern day folk humorists, have hardly attempted to endow him with saintly qualities, preferring instead to focus upon his "earthy humanity." He thus has frequently been portrayed as the zestiest king of *merri olde* England; a charismatic ruler, capable of inspiring immense loyalty from his subjects, with whom he was often known to romp and frolic during an era when knighthood was still in flower.

Yet although he was indeed festive, prodigal, and not at all devoid of humor, the fact remains that Henry VIII could also be imperious, overly self-indulgent, egotistical, and a thoroughgoing autocrat. Moreover, he was also somewhat of a hypocrite, fashioning himself even in

his youth to be a bastion of Catholic orthodoxy, despite
his penchant for lascivious entertainment and the company of wanton females.

It was probably this distorted self-image which
prompted him in 1521 to react to some minor Lutheran
murmerings, emanating from the vicinity of Cambridge
University, by publishing a book entitled *Assertio
septum Sacramentorum* (Defense of the Seven Sacraments). This royal affirmation so pleased Pope Leo X
(whose Catholicism was about exemplary as Henry's),
that the pontiff quickly awarded his newly discovered
Christian soldier the imposing title of *Defensor Fidei*
(Defender of the Faith).

Six years later however, the vicissitudinous King of
England embarked upon a course of action that would
eventually prove him to be far more than simply a duti-
ful pawn on a Papal chessboard. At this time Henry VIII
decided that he wanted to dissolve his seventeen year
marriage with Catherine of Aragon; and in order to do
this, he had to persuade the new Pope, Clement VII, to
grant him an annulment. (A "divorce" was of course an
impossibility since in the Catholic Church marriage was
considered to be a sacrament and therefore inviolable.)

Henry had several reasons for taking this step. The
official one was Biblical in nature. Since Catherine had
previously been the wife of his dead brother, Arthur, he
maintained that although a Pope had granted him
proper authorization, he had nevertheless offended God
by marrying the widowed Spanish princess. To support
his contention, the King of England, who was somewhat
of an amateur theologian, pointed to Chapter XX, verse
21 of the Book of Leviticus, which stated: " . . . if a
man shall take his brother's wife, it is an unclean
thing. . . . They shall remain childless." Henry therefore
declared that Divine Wrath accounted for the fact that
of all Catherine's children, only one (and a female at
that) had survived.

A second reason for Henry's desire to have the Pope declare his marriage null and void arose from his determination to have a son inherit the throne of England. The vexatious memory of the Wars of the Roses served to remind the King that the Tudor dynasty, of which he was but the second to occupy the throne, was in no way the closest to the old royal line. Only a male heir could, in his opinion, safely settle the question of succession; while on the other hand there was every reason for him to believe that should his daughter, Mary, attempt to rule as queen, she could expect no happier fate than that of Matilda, the unfortunate daughter of Henry I.

Finally, Henry had become infatuated with the buxom Anne Boleyn, one of the ladies-in-waiting to the Queen. Refusing to become his mistress, Anne, who was influenced by her ambitious relatives, helped convince Henry that all his interests would be better served if he were to rid himself of Catherine and make her his Queen.

By the beginning of 1527 Henry was ready to initiate proceedings against his Spanish wife. Moreover, in all probability he expected to encounter little difficulty in persuading Clement VII to agree to annul his marriage, since many other Popes—some of them, infinitely corruptible—had performed similar favors for other European sovereigns who based their requests upon only the flimsiest evidence.

Unfortunately, the King of England had chosen the wrong time to cashier his wife and the wrong man to help him do it. The time was inauspicious because 1527 was the year in which Rome was sacked by imperial troops, which were still occupying the Eternal City, when Henry approached Clement VII to put an end to his mésalliance. The commander of the imperial troops, none other than Emperor Charles V, was also King of Spain and even more importantly a nephew of Catherine of Aragon. Since Charles was incensed at the treatment of his aunt by a man he considered to be little more than a royal buffoon; the Pope, who was virtually his prisoner, did not feel inclined to further antagonize this uninvited guest by finding in favor of the King of England.

The man whom Henry chose to secure his annulment was the Papal legate in England, Cardinal Wolsey, a pompous, inflated protagonist of royal supremacy. Such an ally, Henry could well have done without; for although Wolsey was a man of great ability, his high-handed, arrogant ways quickly convinced the Pope to deny his important request that he, as legate in England, be appointed sole judge in the annulment proceedings.

Instead Clement charged Cardinal Campeggio with this responsibility, privately giving him instructions to come to no decision whatever until he received further orders, (which would never come). The sorry affair therefore dragged on for two frustrating years, after which Campeggio adjourned the annulment court for the summer of 1529 without delivering any verdict. Moreover, when the court was due to resume its sessions, His Holiness shocked and enraged the King of England by ordering it to conduct all subsequent proceedings inside the city of Rome, where it could easily be intimidated by the armies of Charles V.

This unexpected turn of events prompted Henry to discharge Wolsey and initiate a series of measures that would culminate in the complete subjugation of the English Church by the crown. It should be noted immediately however that since Henry considered himself to be a pious Catholic until the day he died, the break with Rome would not be utilized to introduce Reformation theology into his realm. Nothing could have been further from his mind. Instead his efforts were mustered simply to achieve the goal of placing himself in *political* control of the Church of England; and in this endeavor, Henry received the enthusiastic support of the majority of his subjects.

As a matter of fact, for a multitude of reasons, both Parliament and most of the public were as anxious as the King himself to set up an independent national Church. As was the case with the Germans, the English had a strong tradition of anti-Papalism, dating back to the early thirteenth century, when King John was forced to deliver England as a fief to Innocent III. In the next century the English monarchy went to appreciable lengths to protect Wycliffe from persecution as a heretic by the Church. Subsequently, English kings steadfastly refused to allow the Inquisition to function inside their realm. Virtually every English sovereign and subject resented the continual Papal attempts to meddle with internal affairs by instituting special taxes and setting up ecclesiastical tribunals.

Furthermore, the spiritual and moral condition of the English episcopacy was highly irreligious, to say the least. Secular priests were for the most part sunk in penury and ignorance, while the regular clergy possessed a not undeserved reputation for indulging themselves in such hedonistic delights as habitual drunkeness and concubinage. Above all, the Church was very affluent; and it appeared to many observers that large parcels of choice land were simply being wasted by the notorious monasteries and nunneries that dotted the map of England.

It therefore requires little imagination to see that in his attempt to subjugate the English Church, Henry VIII hardly emerged as an ogre. Even before the break with Rome, he had already managed to achieve a significant degree of popularity as a wise and foresighted monarch who was steadily removing his realm from the horrid days of Lancaster, York, and the Wars of the Roses. Moreover, his use of the Court of Requests, where the lowly and oftentimes forgotten Englishman could be heard, made him a favorite with the common folk. Thus, from beginning to end, the measures instituted by this charismatic, albeit self-indulgent and hypocritical, ruler, which ultimately led to the establishment of the independent "Henrician Church," were generally hailed with flourishes of patriotic enthusiasm.

In February 1531 the process began with Henry's successful obtainment of the Canterbury Convocation's consent to the formula: "We recognize His Majesty as the only protector, the sole and supreme lord, and, as far as Christ's law allows, the supreme head of the Church and the clergy of England." Consequently, before the year was over, the King felt sufficiently secure in position to decree that Catherine of Aragon be removed from court with or without Papal acquiescence.

In May 1532 the English clergy renounced its legislative power and abandoned Church government to the King, all of which paved the way for the final blow against Rome, officially called the Act in Restraint of Appeals. Promulgated in 1533, this decree completely obliterated the Pope's jurisdiction in England and allowed the court of the Archbishop of Canterbury to function as the supreme ecclesiastical tribunal. Then, in May of the same year, Thomas Cranmer, a married clergyman with pronounced Reformation leanings, who had just been appointed to the see of Canterbury, declared the marriage between Henry and Catherine of Aragon null and void. Four months later, Anne Boleyn gave birth, not to the hoped for boy, but to the future Queen Elizabeth. Finally, the inevitable reaction came from Rome, as Clement VII excommunicated the King of England in July 1533.

* * * * *

If one were to speculate upon the justification for the many decrees of excommunication that were promulgated by sixteenth century Popes against Reformation leaders, one might well conclude that the one directed at Henry is the easiest to defend. Even the most rigid

Catholic would have to admit that in the formation of
the separatist movements launched by Calvin, Zwingli,
Luther, and the majority of Anabaptist leaders, considerations of personal conscience and dogmatics played a
definitive role. But on the other hand, although the second Tudor monarch dabbled in the Book of Leviticus to
explain his actions, the end product was more of a ra-
tionalization than a justification. Moreover, the fact that
a mere three years elapsed between the time of Henry's
second marriage to that of Anne Boleyn's execution by
sovereign decree, casts more suspicion upon the nature
of his original intentions. Finally, when one considers
that before the King breathed his last, he married four
more women for a grand total of six; it is difficult indeed to imagine how this rather insatiable chap could
ever hope to audition successfully for a halo. It is no
wonder that Martin Luther himself regarded Henry as
little more than a venal autocrat who forced his subjects
to swallow whatever dogmas he found it convenient to
espouse at a given moment.

Yet the fact remains that whether he is deserving of
praise or damnation, Henry VIII did become for all
practical purposes the "Supreme Head" of the Church
of England; and once placed in this position, he worked
very efficiently to consolidate his gains. Confirmation of
the King's new power and prerogatives came in 1534
with the enactment of the Act of Supremacy which re-
stated more forcefully and succinctly than ever before
his right to be "taken, accepted, and reputed the only
supreme head on earth of the Church of England." With
this law, Henry had a *carte blanche* to manage every
aspect of ecclesiastical business in any way he saw fit.

Playing upon the extravagance and corruption of the
monastic system, Henry, working primarily through his
loyal servant Thomas Cromwell, dissolved every English
monastery and nunnery. Precious metals, jewels, stained
glass windows, building materials, and Church lands

were confiscated and sold. Quite characteristically, Henry did not use the money that he thus acquired to care for the poor (who were now virtually without a reliable source of charity). Instead, most of the booty and land was sold to the petty nobility in order to endear their sovereign to them and enlist their support against a Roman Catholic restoration. Subsequent events proved Henry to have been substantially correct in these tactics, as the English landed gentry gave consistent support and encouragement to the Tudor House and the new Anglican Church, no matter what character it assumed.

Moreover, resistance to all of Henry's anti-Roman policies was in general meager, to say the very least. During his reign, there was only one truly mass protest against the English crown, that of the Pilgrimage of Grace, whose advocates demanded a return to "normalcy." The rising was quickly and systematically crushed (and although similar disturbances would break out in future years, they also would be handled with equal facility by Elizabeth I).

Individuals who refused to acknowledge the legality of Henry's marriage to Anne Boleyn were rapidly liquidated. John Fisher, the Bishop of Rochester, who had been the major supporter of Catherine of Aragon during the annulment hearings, was executed in June 1535. Sir Thomas More, the reputed "Man for all seasons," royal chancellor after the disgrace of Wolsey, and incidentally an inveterate heretic-hunter in his own right, lost the battle to retain the use of his head in July of the same year. Finally, about fifty Franciscans were sent to prison for the rest of their lives, while the Carthusians of London were forced to experience the ignominious traitors' death.

Once firmly established as the ruler of the new Church of England, Henry did not see fit to tolerate any Protestant sects within his realm. On the contrary, in 1539 he induced Parliament to pass the "Act for Abol-

ishing Diversity of Opinion." Containing the famous Six
Articles, this law reaffirmed religious practices that Protestants found to be totally repugnant. Transubstantiation, clerical celibacy, auricular confession, and private
masses would remain integral parts of the Anglican
Church. To protest against this state of affairs was treason.

On 28 July 1540 Henry turned on his right-hand
man, the now-Protestant Thomas Cromwell, sending this
poor devil to the scaffold as a convicted traitor! Two
days later three priests were hanged for treason because
they denied Henry's supremacy, while three Protestants
were burned at the stake because they were judged to be
heretics. On 4 August three more Catholics were
brutally executed on a charge of treason. Finally
Anabaptists were hunted down like dogs. In May 1535
fourteen were burned at the stake. Dozens more shared
this gruesome fate in 1538 and 1540.

Yet when the balance sheet of persecution is carefully
scrutinized, an interesting observation can be made. Although Henry considered himself an exemplary Catholic
to the very end of his life, he nevertheless allowed the
married Lutheran-sympathizer, Thomas Cranmer, to remain Archbishop of Canterbury. He also eschewed pun-
ishing Bishop Latimer for his firm Protestant convic-
tions, merely requesting that the prelate prematurely
resign from his episcopal office. Furthermore, he endorsed the use of the new English Bible, which had been
prepared and translated by such outspoken Reformers
as Tyndale and Coverdale.

Protestants might then with great justification have
moaned and groaned under Henry's yoke; yet the fact
remained that by the end of his reign, the ground had
been well prepared for a truly religious Reformation to
follow upon the heels of his political break with Rome.
This was virtually assured by one of Henry's final
acts, which provided his young male heir with a

regency council that contained a preponderance of
Protestant talent.

* * * * *

In 1547 the nine year old son of Henry VIII and
Lady Jane Seymour became King Edward VI and began
a six year reign. Before his premature death the Protestant Reformation acquired a significant number of English followers, coming generally from urban areas and
quite often consisting of the most inspired, articulate
Christians. Presiding over the spread of Protestantism
were Edward Seymour, the Duke of Somerset
(1547-49), and John Dudley, the Earl of Warwick and
subsequently Duke of Northumberland (1549-53).

Somerset, a skilled and tactful uncle of the King,
wanted very much to deliver the entire realm into the
Protestant fold; but quite characteristically he strongly
preferred to achieve this goal with as little coercion as
possible. He repealed the Act for Abolishing Diversity of
Opinion as well as Henry's statutes against heresy, re-
placing them with the more conciliatory Act of Uniformity. This provided England with a blueprint for religious conformity, based on the first Book of Common
Prayer.

One author has quite rightly pointed out that as a
guide to ecclesiastical practice, the prayer book was an
exercise in ambiguity. Yet this was no accident. Somerset felt that the only way to build up a consensus in the
national church was to allow as many Englishmen as
possible to "do their own thing" religiously if this
would merely conform to certain, highly generalized
formulations. And, major events of a subsequent reign
would demonstrate the soundness of the Duke's tactics.
Unfortunately, well before Somerset's conciliatory policies could be adequately tested at mid-century, his
regency government collapsed under the impact of a
coup engineered by his rival, John Dudley, who shortly
thereafter sent him to the gallows.

Northumberland, a master of court intrigue who was
at best a fair-weather Protestant, took advantage of
domestic economic unrest to seize power in the autumn
of 1549. During this year ruinous inflation and the effects of the enclosure movement motivated a number of
poverty-stricken farmers from Norfolk to organize
themselves into what became known as Kett's Rebellion. Once Somerset indicated his sympathy with the
plight of these rebels, Northumberland denounced him
as a traitor. Then summoning all his Machiavellian talents, the unscrupulous Duke gained the support of certain Catholic nobles in his illicit bid for power by
promising to compensate these Papist chumps with the
restoration of the Roman Church in England.

Nothing of course could have been further from his
mind since Northumberland had for some time been
casting his greedy eyes upon the remaining assets of the
Catholic Church. Once in power he plundered its build-
ings, using the jewels and precious metals that were confiscated to pay some royal debts but mainly to make
himself filthy rich.

Under his iron rule even the bishops of the Henrician
Church were deposed and cast into prison. Catholics
who refused to participate in new religious services were
either fined or incarcerated. The burning of Anabaptists,
which had ceased during Somerset's regime, was once
again in season.

Since Northumberland cared little about purely
doctrinal matters, Cranmer was given the green light to
assert himself in a manner about which he previously
could merely dream. With the help of some eminent
continental reformers, the Archbishop of Canterbury
composed a new, more Protestant Book of Common
Prayer, which by a second Act of Uniformity (1552)
was thrust upon every English clergyman. Moreover, in
his unpublished *Reformatio legum ecclesiasticarum*,
Cranmer established the most severe penalties for those
individuals whom he cared to designate as heretics.

During the Northumberland ascendancy, tyrannical Erastianism was accompanied by rather senseless acts of government-sponsored vandalism. Inside what had formerly been Catholic Churches, beautiful altars were smashed to bits and replaced by communion tables. Sanctuaries were plastered up. Priceless, old liturgical books were burned, as Parliament presided over a new orgy of iconoclasm that continued until the tubercular King finally coughed his last in July 1553.

Previous to his death Edward VI had assigned the crown to Lady Jane Grey, a daughter of his cousin, Frances Grey. In so doing he tried to exclude Mary and Elizabeth, the two remaining legitimate children of Henry VIII, from their birthright. Lady Jane, an accomplished scholar with little genuine desire to become queen, acceded to the King's wishes and dutifully married Northumberland's son. However, when the proclamation of Lady Jane as queen by her father-in-law met with no response, all parties to the displacement scheme were arrested. The nefarious Northumberland received his just desserts in August and was followed to the scaffold five months later by the would-be royal couple. Mary Tudor, a pious, sincere, but rather bigoted Roman Catholic, now became Queen of England.

* * * * *

In general the daughter of Henry VIII and Catherine of Aragon has been the recipient of an unfavorable historical commentary, all of which has inspired a certain whiskey-splashing connoisseur to immortalize her in a potent concoction that has become known as a "Bloody Mary." Moreover, her image has hardly been improved by the sentimental apologias, written by certain, inspired Catholic historians who have attempted to portray this unhappy woman as the star-crowned queen of the apocalypse.

In all fairness to Mary, it should be remembered that

she wished to restore Catholicism to England in a far more peaceful way than that which was used by her father, Northumberland, and even the prudent Somerset to bring about and maintain the break with Rome. Less than two weeks after she was enthusiastically welcomed by the city of London as the new English sovereign, Mary declared that she had no intention of hindering or doing violence to the conscience of others. In mid-August 1553 the Catholic queen proclaimed that "she willeth and strictly chargeth and commandeth all her good loving subjects to live together in quiet and Christian charity, leaving those new-found devilish terms of papist and heretic and such like. . . . "

Advised by Bishop Gardiner and Cardinal Pole to rule moderately, Mary induced Parliament to pass the Act of Repeal, which gave legal status to Papal bulls, but only if they did not conflict with English laws and royal dignity. Moreover, under her sponsorship the treason laws of Henry VIII and Edward VI were repealed. Finally, Mary agreed that those Englishmen, coming mainly from the gentry class, who acquired Church lands during the Reformation years would be allowed to retain them.

Unfortunately, Mary insisted on marrying Philip II of Spain, a partisan of the most intense Catholicism and a monarch who was unpopular even in his own country. In so doing the Queen seemed to be selling English national interests down the river, and she quickly proved to be not at all unwilling to make her subjects into pawns of Spanish foreign policy.

This marriage made the more radical English Protestants, who viewed the Anglo-Spanish rapprochement with horror, appear to be super-patriots. A fanatical minority of these Reformation enthusiasts engaged in criminal, outrageous, and seditious activities; and in so doing never missed an opportunity to ridicule and villify the Queen. Mary's reaction was to revive the old laws against heresy, a feat which she accomplished with Parliamentary consent in December 1554. From this date to the end of her reign, 273 "heretics" were executed. There is no way to excuse the Queen for this slaughter. Yet it ought to be pointed out that her successor, Elizabeth I, albeit in the course of a longer reign, legally murdered about the same number of people. (The Good Queen Bess was simply more careful in her actions and enjoyed the services of highly skilled public relations men.)

Moreover, the exasperating torrents of abuse, slander, and character assassinations that Mary had to endure at the hands of such radical emigrés as John Knox and Christopher Goodman drove the hyperemotional Queen to take more stringent measures against those whom she supposed to be the enemies of herself, her husband, and Roman Catholicism. Safe in German and Swiss sanctuaries, Knox and his colleagues "bravely" aimed their most poisonous shafts at the Queen, whom they self-righteously damned when such actions inevitably aggravated her persecution activities.

Attesting to the critical position in which English Protestants found themselves as a result of Knox's impetuous ebullience, another emigré, named David Whitehead, wrote a rather revealing letter to Calvin in September 1555. In it Whitehead complained about Knox's unnecessarily antagonistic pamphlet, *An Admonition to Christians*, in the following way: "This we can assure you, that that outrageous pamphlet of Knox's added much oil to the flame of persecution in England. For before the publication of that book not one of our brethren had suffered death; but as soon as it came forth, we doubt not but that you are well aware of the number of excellent men who have perished in the flames."

The flames about which Whitehead spoke were the fires at Smithfield, in which the heretic Bishops of

Gloucester and London died by order of the Queen. Thomas Cranmer and Hugh Latimer were executed in the same brutal way. However, even more important than the demise of these ecclesiastical bigwigs was the fact that large numbers of ordinary Englishmen, who had the sympathy of their peers, were also burned at the stake. This enabled the English Protestant movement to claim popular support in a way that it had not been able to during the preceding reign.

Mary Tudor died in November 1558, leaving her realm in an incredible mess. The Spanish alliance had hurt England considerably. Not only did it grind national pride right into the dust, it also involved the island kingdom in an ill-advised and costly war against France, which resulted in the destruction of the last English stronghold on the continent. The all-important navy had fallen into disrepair, laying England open to foreign invasion. Despite the fact that the currency had been repeatedly debased, the royal treasury was bone dry. Finally, the realm was bordering on religious chaos: Catholics versus Protestants, Erastians versus Ultramontanists.

The lamentable condition of France during the same year has already been described in a previous chapter of this study. Suffice it to say that to the average Englishman, the Kingdom of Henry II appeared to be virtually invulnerable. Whether England would solve its many problems, all of which were intertwined, depended on the ability of the next sovereign, the celebrated Elizabeth I.

* * * * *

The daughter of Henry VIII and Anne Boleyn was a truly remarkable woman, perhaps the only Tudor who could have kept the English ship of state afloat in an age of wars, rebellions, economic dislocation, religious and political strife. From the age of three, at which time her mother was beheaded for allegedly committing adultery, Elizabeth led a life, so full of dangers and adversity, that by her twenty-first birthday she had received a political education worthy of the most seasoned Renaissance realist.

The tall, red-haired highly imaginative monarch had also been the beneficiary of an excellent conventional education, which gave her exceptional training in foreign languages. Her linguistic ability enabled Elizabeth to exercise significant control over English diplomatic affairs, as she freely spoke with foreign ambassadors in Latin, French, and Italian. Moreover, she was a glutton for work, as were the truly first-rate advisors with whom she chose to surround herself. Few English civil servants have ever been able to match the ability and loyalty of Cecil, Walsingham, and Hatton.

In 1558 Elizabeth knew she had to revitalize the sagging English economy; re-establish royal prestige that had sunk to a dangerous level during the previous reign; walk a diplomatic tightrope amid a very unfavorable constellation of European states; and above all work out a settlement that would prevent a religious civil war from breaking out in her realm. The Queen succeeded on all counts.

The economy received its needed shot in the arm through the application of mercantilistic measures that would have impressed Louis XIV a century later. It was further strengthened by inducing thousands of gifted textile workers to emigrate from the strife-torn Netherlands to new homes in England, where they taught their skills to the natives.

The prestige of the crown was enhanced by Elizabeth's success in convincing the average Englishmen that she had his best interests constantly in mind. She maintained continual personal contact with even her most humble subjects, whom she refused to forget when they became too old or poverty-stricken to fend for themselves.

Moreover, she was able to control Parliament in a way that her successors never could. Sometimes its members were intimidated and steamrollered by her. Other times Elizabeth would not hesitate to appear quivering before them with tears in her eyes, exclaiming that she was only a poor defenseless woman who needed the chivalric, intrepid Parliamentarians to help her care for the bleeding realm. In either case, the Queen usually got her way.

Diplomatically, she always kept her lines open. Elizabeth was usually more than a match for foreign ambassadors whom she mesmerized, misled, and promised the impossible. A consummate practitioner of the art of procrastination, she kept a number of important suitors on the string until she finally felt it safe to refuse to get married, in no less than nine different languages! Not until English domestic affairs and external defenses were sufficiently stable would the prudent Queen yield an inch to popular demands to strike out against her major enemies.

It was however in the matter of religious policy that Elizabeth experienced her finest hours; and although luck was certainly on her side, the fact remains that without her skill and fortitude, the all-important consensus for the Church of England would never have been secured. Strangely enough, despite the Marian persecutions, it would not at all have been impossible for Elizabeth to retain Catholicism as the official faith of her realm, provided she would agree to abandon the Protestant pogroms. Moreover, the Pope would in all probability have recognized the semi-independent nature of the Anglican Church by granting Elizabeth the same type of arrangement that was accorded to Francis I in 1516 by the Concordat of Bologna. And in view of the weakened condition of the English defense system, it would not at all have been unreasonable to suppose that the new Queen might embrace Catholicism in order to deprive the Kings of France and Spain of an obvious excuse to attack and probably successfully invade her realm.

In any event it was not obvious at the beginning of Elizabeth's reign what her ecclesiastical policy would be. In the first public document which she produced, an "et cetera" was strategically put at the end of Elizabeth's titles. This replaced the official designation of "Supreme Head of the Church," that was used by Henry VIII and Edward VI. The resultant ambiguity left most English subjects and the entire Catholic world speculating about the future. The first declaration of William Cecil, the new Secretary of State, forbade under stringent penalties any change whatever in religious affairs. Elizabeth inveigled the fanatical and pugnacious Pope Paul IV by retaining Mary's ambassador to the Vatican and promising to send a blue-ribbon embassy in the near future. In her private chapel Catholic Masses continued to be celebrated.

Yet as the months passed, with Elizabeth gaining confidence that her hold on the throne was becoming sufficiently secure, she began to reflect upon the irresolvable conflict between papal supremacy and English nationalism. The new Queen also became keenly aware of the great advantages which she could enjoy presiding over a strong monarchy with complete control of the Church and its servants. Consequently, Elizabeth submitted two key bills to Parliament, which were voted upon and passed by the end of April 1559: one restored Cranmer's Prayer Book of 1552 and the other revived the Act of Supremacy.

Neither of these bills however was a carbon copy of any previous law. The first, which amounted to a new Act of Uniformity, provided for some modification in the Book of Common Prayer in order to make it acceptable to at least lukewarm Catholics. Elizabeth's idea was to keep its assertions as vague and ambiguous as possible, leaving it up to the individual—Catholic or Protestant—to interpret them as he saw fit. One example should suffice to illustrate the Queen's tactic: When the priest (or minister) delivered the Communion bread to the faithful, he was instructed to say: "The Body of our Lord Jesus Christ, which was given for thee, preserve thy body and soul unto everlasting life. Take and eat this in remembrance that Christ died for thee, and feed on him in thy heart by faith, with thanksgiving." Similarly, in delivering the Communion wine, the priest (or minister) would say: "The Blood of our Lord Jesus Christ, which was shed for thee, preserve thy body and soul unto everlasting life. Drink this in remembrance that Christ's blood was shed for thee, and be thankful." In neither case did the celebrant declare that what he was administering to his congregation *was* the Body or the Blood of Jesus Christ. Then again, he did not say that the bread and wine were *not* the Body and Blood of Jesus Christ.

It was therefore hoped that both Catholics and Protestants, who were officially commanded to assist at state religious services, would do so, but on their own terms. Put another way, without condoning freedom of worship, Elizabeth strove to allow freedom of conscience.

Elizabeth's Act of Supremacy did not correspond exactly to that of her father in at least one important way. Instead of proclaiming the Queen "Supreme Head of the Church of England," it made her only "Supreme Governor . . . of all spiritual and ecclesiastical things." This title was a bit more palatable to Catholics, and more or less acceptable to Calvinists, who had taken exception to Henry VIII's title as an affront to God, the only true "head" of a Church.

Furthermore, although papal authority in England was repudiated, Elizabeth did not abolish the episcopacy, as radical Protestants had hoped. No provisions were immediately made to punish commission of the simple act of heresy. Only those heretics who were judged also to be traitors had to concern themselves with royal displeasure. The requirement that the clergy were to recognize the Queen as Supreme Governor did not seem to have aroused much hostility, since about ninety-seven per cent at least paid lip service to this law. In the early years of Elizabeth's reign almost no attempt was made to enforce conformity of religion. Between 1559 and 1570 no one was put to death for religious considerations. As a matter of fact, the government knew that during these years private celebrations of the Mass were taking place all over the map of England; and it did nothing to prevent this.

In 1563 the Anglican Church received a constitution in the Thirty-nine Articles, which defined its creed in a characteristically evasive tone. Aiming at a compromise between Catholicism and the important professions of faith, which had been produced by the Reformation, it on the one hand rejected such Roman forms and practices as the Latin liturgy, auricular confession, clerical celibacy, and of course allegiance to the Pope. Yet, on the other hand, it denied justification by faith, the priesthood of all believers, and Zwinglian symbolism.

Elizabeth's court contained ardent Calvinists as well as crypto-Catholics; and although the former were officially Anglicans, they nevertheless wanted to "purify" the Church of England. These Puritans, as they were called, not only formed an opposition block to the Queen from within the national Church itself; they also gradually gained appreciable power in the Parliament. Therefore, to retain the loyalty of both ends of the religious spectrum, Elizabeth could never abandon her middle of the road policies, which like most compromises completely pleased no one.

Catholic sympathizers were not satisfied with the retention of merely the forms of their worship, which they felt consisted of more than caps, copes, surplices, and incense. They also resented the inevitable harassment from Cecil and Walsingham that had to be endured during those many times when England was threatened by Catholic enemies.

The Puritans demanded the right to reform the structure of the Anglican Church on a Calvinistic model and therefore to abolish such Catholic carryovers as the offices of Archbishop, Archdeacon, Lord Bishop, and the Commissary's Court. They also wanted to purge the Book of Common Prayer, which in their words was "an unperfect book, culled and picked out of that Popish dunghill, the Mass-book, full of abominations." Yet Elizabeth refused to waver in her contention that the only manageable religious settlement was a comprehensive one. In order to survive, the Anglican Church had to be a broad or "latitudinarian" institution.

Although her success in inducing the majority of Englishmen to worship in the national church was a direct function of her brilliance and administrative ability, it is nonetheless true that the goddess, Fortuna, deigned to smile upon the Queen. In 1559 the potentially most strenuous opponents to the establishment of the Anglican Church were Catholic bishops, sixteen of whom traditionally presided over the dioceses of England. However, at this time sixty per cent of the sees happened to be vacant. Moreover, the parish clergy, on the whole, were not inclined to offer any open resistance to Elizabeth's ecclesiastical changes; and this was perhaps due as much to their apathy and abysmal ignorance as to her judicious manner of presiding over the religious transformation.

Lay as well as clerical leadership was lacking to English Catholics from the beginning of Elizabeth's reign. In 1559 Oxford and Cambridge experienced a mass exodus

of some three hundred deans, fellows, and assorted
scholars, all of whom were members of the Catholic
Church. To make matters worse for the ancient faith,
during the critical Parliamentary sessions of the same
year, those non-Protestant nobles who bothered to show
up at all voted in accordance with government wishes.
Under these circumstances, the average Catholic generally had to rely upon his own conscience to tell him
how far he could follow the new laws. The only one
which immediately affected himself and his fellow reli-
gionists was the regulation that obliged everyone to be
present in his parish church on Sundays and Holy Days
of Obligation. If he and his family refused to attend the
prescribed religious services, they would all be fined a
shilling for every absence.

Since most Englishmen could not afford to pay at
this rate for the luxury of maintaining a strict Catholic
conscience, they gradually allowed themselves to sit in
church, where they listened to psalms, with which they
were already familiar, and recited prayers that were
mainly translations of the collects used in their own
parish churches for hundreds of years. With little effort
they could sleep through the sermon unless the rector
were either educated or a zealot; and since the new
Communion service took place only about four times a
year, it was generally not a major source of anxiety.

If the average English Catholic living in 1559 possessed any knowledge of his faith as it existed before
Henry VIII's break with Rome, the thirty chaotic years
which followed this rupture would almost certainly have
all but obliterated this cognition. Moreover, the majority of the uninspired Catholic clergy of 1559 could
hardly have clearly remembered the normal Catholic life
of three decades past with its various acts, rites, and
ceremonies. In any case, if a man had been a priest
during Wolsey's time, the chances are he would have
been dead by 1559, since during the sixteenth century,
sexagenerians were a rarity, to say the least.

Most of the priests, who *were* living during the early years of Elizabeth's reign, had at least once publicly sworn their repudiation of the Pope; and those who had not actually preached on the topic of Papal degeneracy were nevertheless quite imbued with the thoughts of their superiors on this matter. These clergymen had almost exclusively been trained on the doctrines of Cranmer's prayer books, which superficially bore a stronger resemblance to Catholic dogma than to that of the Reformation. Therefore, they could rationalize their somewhat opportunistic adherence to the so-called Bishop's Book and King's Book, by maintaining that the teachings found in these "holy volumes" were simply those of England's answer to French Gallicanism.

Quite fortunately for Elizabeth then, her average Catholic subject attempted to combine with his old beliefs the doctrines of the Anglican Church. Some Catholics even decided to receive the new Communion, which would be administered to them by their own priests, who also continued to celebrate Catholic Masses. English Catholicism drifted along in this way for about eleven years until Pius V finally excommunicated Elizabeth, hoping that such a papal clarification of the Queen's religious status would at this late date rouse the countryside against her. But the Pope's tactic quite understandably failed to achieve the expected results. England by 1570 had ceased being a country in which the mass of people were desirous to be Catholics.

In subsequent years Catholic activists tried to discipline what was left of their Church in England to roll back the Anglican tide. William Allen, who left the country in 1565 to escape persecution, spent the remainder of his life organizing seminaries and missions from the European continent. Made a cardinal in 1587, Allen became generally recognized as leader of the English Catholics and usually managed to bridge the gap between members of the regular and secular clergy.

However, seven years later His Eminence died and

was not followed by any leader who could equal him in either moral influence or official importance. To make matters worse, during the next twenty years continental Jesuits insisted on monkeying with the internal affairs of the English Catholic Church. One such character named Robert Persons S.J. wrote a far-fetched book, entitled *A Conference About the Next Succession to the Crown of England*, which put forward the candidacy of Isabella, the daughter of the Spanish King! Not only did the book infuriate the English government, which consequently stepped up its harassment of the Catholic population; it also led the secular Catholic clergy to conclude that all Jesuits were simply puppets of the King of Spain and possibly even traitors to the best interests of all good Englishmen. Needless to say Elizabeth's government carefully exploited these differences among the Catholic priesthood.

* * * * *

In 1570 Pius V was not simply content with excommunicating the Queen of England. Acting in a fashion which was similar to that of certain of his romantic predecessors, for example: Gregory VII, Innocent III, Innocent IV, and John XXII, he pompously declared Elizabeth deposed. As one author has put it, "out of date and ineffective, the papal sentence became in the hands of the Queen a terrible weapon against her Catholic subjects." The weapon became even more dreadful when Elizabeth decided to react furiously against the many diabolical plans and schemes that were launched in order to make the Pope's deposition effective.

Pius V, Gregory XIII, and Sixtus V along with Philip II, the Society of Jesus, English Roman Catholics, and Mary Queen of Scots together and separately hatched a continual series of plots against the life of the Queen. None of them worked however because of their utter stupidity as well as the fact that Elizabeth's secret service, under the very capable Francis Walsingham, would immediately discover the existence of these political abortions before they even took form. Reacting to the Bull of Excommunication and the first assassination attempts, the English government reinterpreted its treason laws. As of 1571 the death penalty would be given to any "traitor" who dared to say that the Queen was an imposter, a heretic, or a schismatic. A decade later the persecution became even worse, as the government decided to move against the Catholic missionaries and two leading Jesuit "troublemakers," Edmund Campion and Robert Persons.

In July 1580 a royal proclamation ordered all parents who were having their children brought up abroad, without the express permission of the government, to recall them within four months. In addition it ordered all subjects to denounce English Jesuits and other missionaries who had secretly returned home to proselytize. During the next year Parliament decreed that anyone who persuaded an Anglican to return to Catholicism or who had himself been reconverted was guilty of treason and therefore liable to the death penalty. In December 1581 Campion and two other priests fell victims to Parliament's new law, while Persons barely managed to flee England a few steps ahead of Walsingham's human bloodhounds.

Meanwhile, subsequent legislation raised the fine that Catholics had to pay, should they decide not to attend official worship services. After 1581 any priest who said Mass was also subject to a heavy fine plus one year's imprisonment, while half of this penalty would be meted out to those individuals who dared to attend such a religious celebration.

In 1585 a new law was enacted by Parliament stating that any priest who had been ordained on the European continent after 1559 was obliged to leave England within forty days. Those who remained without pledging their allegiance to the Queen would be committing high treason. Foreign priests who for whatever reason found themselves on English soil had to take the oath of supremacy within three days of their arrival or run the risk of execution. Whoever gave aid or comfort to recalcitrant priests was guilty of committing a felony.

Showing its utter contempt for the abilities of the old Marian clergy and preferring not to create a host of unnecessary martyrs, the government did not subject these priests to the law of 1585. Elizabeth felt moreover that in a matter of a few years any cleric who had been ordained during the reign of her half-sister would be dead. It is no wonder that once the measures of the 1580's had been put into effect, Walsingham could with tongue in cheek write the French ambassador that his Queen had no intention of compelling consciences in any way. By the end of Elizabeth's reign 189 Catholics had been executed. Forty more had been cast into prison, where they subsequently died.

* * * * *

As Elizabeth grew older, she became progressively less inclined to tolerate Protestant, as well as Catholic, deviations from the national church. In her opinion the most obnoxious Reformation sects were those of the Anabaptists and anti-Trinitarians, both of which were, as early as 1561, ordered to leave the realm. During the next decade, many of the hated sectarians, who chose to ignore the royal directive, were rounded up and imprisoned or burned at the stake. As had been the case during the reigns of Henry VIII and Edward VI, little mercy was shown to these spiritual pilgrims who had adopted a method of worship with which the religious establishment could not sympathize and therefore decided to destroy.

By 1570 the Presbyterian wing of the Puritan movement became organized under the leadership of Thomas

Cartwright, a dynamic Cambridge theologian who would prove to be a most troublesome thorn in the side of Queen. The Presbyterians, while maintaining their loyalty to the Anglican Church, nevertheless declared that it had become worldly and corrupt. Therefore, they advocated the institution of measures which would purify and perhaps even return the church to the pristine condition that it had enjoyed in apostolic times. In a series of lectures which he gave on the Acts of the Apostles, Cartwright echoed the old Puritan demand for a complete reform of the Book of Common Prayer, while also maintaining the need to abolish the episcopacy of the Anglican Church. When John Whitgift, the Chancellor of Cambridge University, accused Cartwright of trying to separate himself and his followers from the national church, the latter protested that he simply wanted to reform it. The renegade theologian further proclaimed that he sought conformity to the Church with as much vigor and determination as did the Queen herself. Of course, what he had in mind was a Puritan conformity.

Rightly believing that Presbyterianism would constitute a serious threat to her own powers and prerogatives, Elizabeth reacted adversely to what she described as the pious platitudes of the radical Cambridge theologian. In one of her appearances before Parliament she thundered: "[Such reforms] lead to intolerable innovation; they lack divine authority; they effect an unspeakable tyranny; they are most dangerous to all good Christian government."

In 1571 Elizabeth drove through Parliament a stricter Act of Uniformity, which dismissed some of the more radical Puritan ministers. Two years later all Puritan pamphlets were suppressed. In the autumn of 1573 all Anglican bishops were ordered to muzzle and punish every outspoken Puritan in their dioceses. In 1583 Elizabeth appointed Chancellor Whitgift to become Archbishop of Canterbury and shortly thereafter admitted this Anglican martinet, (whom she would call her "black husband"), to the Privy Council.

Cartwright immediately lost his position at Cambridge and averted a subsequent attempt to imprison him only by fleeing to Germany. Meanwhile, Whitgift commanded the entire Anglican clergy to endorse the following declarations: 1. The Queen possesses supreme power in the Church of England. 2. The Book of Common Prayer contains nothing that is contrary to the Word of God. 3. The whole of the Thirty-nine Articles is in accordance with the Word of God. Two hundred ministers who refused to obey the Archbishop of Canterbury were informed that their services would no longer be considered desirable.

In October 1588 England was surprised by the appearance of a Puritan counterattack taking the form of a highly irreverent pamphlet, written by an individual who called himself Martin Marprelate, and printed "oversea in Europe, within two furlongs of a Bouncing Priest." This tract, containing the most carping satire ever directed against the Anglican episcopacy, was quickly followed by three more equally sardonic broadsides.

By the time the enraged government tracked down the apostate printing presses, four more "Martins" had appeared, demanding the "fumigation" of the Anglican Church and the castigation of the Queen. By the end of 1590 however, the propaganda conspiracy was completely uncovered and the ringleaders brutally punished, three of them paying with their lives, another being condemned to spend his remaining days in prison. Moreover, the Queen took advantage of the hysteria created by the Marprelate tracts and a subsequent abortive rising, inspired by three religious maniacs, to harass any Presbyterian or nonconforming Calvinist, whom she had wanted to proceed against but heretofore could not, due to a lack of incriminating evidence. Now Elizabeth

simply accused such individuals of sympathizing with
the recent disturbances; and before they knew what hit
them, they were in jail. Cartwright, for example, who
had recently returned to England and was totally innocent of any involvement in either the Marprelate affair
or the pseudo-revolution was obliged to cool his heels
for eighteen months. According to one author, before
Whitgift terminated his crusade, the nascent Presbyterian order, which had by 1590 spread itself into approximately twenty English counties, was destroyed,
and all of its leaders taken into custody.

* * * * *

When Elizabeth ascended the throne, she supposedly
petitioned God to give her grace to govern with clem-
ency and without bloodshed. Although it can be argued
that the Queen hardly believed in God at all and that
both her Catholic and Nonconformist subjects were oppressed by very rigorous laws, which not infrequently
produced martyrs; the fact remains that during her
reign, England did not have to endure religious civil war
and its resultant horrors.

To some degree Elizabeth was certainly more fortunate in the circumstances surrounding her attempt to
prevent this than were her continental counterparts. The
blessings of English insularity were supplemented by the
absence of princes of the blood, who with semi-
sacrosanct bodies could rival the crown and endow their
ceaseless rebellions with an aura of respectability. With
feudal liberties in virtual ruin, the major English nobles
overspent their reduced incomes on ostentatious attire
and more than adequate housing. Living at the edge of
bankruptcy, they spent less time thinking about war
than about tracking down and marrying somebody's
rich widow.

However, the outward stability of Elizabethan society
in no way obliterated the bitter legacy of the three

previous reigns, in which Anglicans, continental reformers, and Catholics alternated in power—each religious faction taking its turn at exploiting and persecuting its rivals. Moreover, as has already been pointed out,
the moment Elizabeth was excommunicated, it was
open season on her life. Seldom has any ruler had to live
in such continual danger of assassination as did the second daughter of Henry VIII.

Yet this remarkable queen managed to die in bed, at
the end of a reign that spanned nearly half a century.
During her years of power, this woman of the keenest
intelligence and most superlative attributes presided
over an economic boom for her realm, restored the dignity of her crown, and made England into a power that
could once again hold its own in the European state
system.

Above all, Elizabeth skilfully employed a policy
based on compromise, coercion, and conciliation to
work out a viable religious settlement. Twenty years of
these tactics effectively weakened Catholicism and Non-
conformism while creating grave divisions among the
faithful of both persuasions. Conversely, the Queen's
maneuverings enabled her to bring into existence a national church, which gave the appearance of being
"catholic" but not Roman Catholic, Protestant but not
devoid of an episcopacy. Because of the famous Thirty-
nine Articles it became a truly latitudinarian institution,
which permitted religious celebrations to range from
what was nearly a Catholic Mass to a starkly simple
Calvinist service.

Despised by its enemies, warmly endorsed by its supporters, passively accepted by the broad "silent" majority of the realm, the Elizabethan religious settlement
worked. England experienced no St. Bartholemew's Day
Massacre, thanks to its Queen, who guided it along a
path that could well have been appreciated by the
politiques across the Channel. Perhaps the greatest testa-

ment to the magnitude and the achievement of Elizabeth has come from a man who can hardly have been considered as one of her warmer friends, Pope Sixtus V. Shortly after his coronation the pontiff exclaimed: "She certainly is a great queen, and were she only a Catholic she would be our dearly beloved. Just look how well she governs! She is only a woman, only mistress of half an island, and yet she makes herself feared by Spain, France, the Empire, by all."

* * * * *

Summary and Conclusion

The history of Christianity has actually exhibited few protracted periods not characterized by internal ferment and tension. Almost from its inception the Church Universal has been marred by schismatic and heretical movements which are so numerous that one sometimes suspects that there should have been a Reformation before 1517. Yet the fact remains that the edifice of Christianity was hardly cracked by Donatists, Arians, Gnostics, Predestinarians, Hussites, Lollards, Circumcellions, Catharists, Antinomians, Beghards, or similar sectarians.

With the waning of the Middle Ages however the crises continued, and the Church's immunity to them diminished markedly. By 1300 it became clear that the Papacy could no longer assert itself against European kings in the way to which it had been accustomed during previous centuries, when it freely took, as a guide to its political prerogatives, chapter I verse 10 of the Book of Jeremiah:

> See I have this day set thee over nations and over the kingdoms to root out, and to pull down, and to destroy and to overthrow, to build and to plant.

In 1300 Pope Boniface VIII was in the midst of a struggle with Philip IV of France, in which the former mustered all his unremitting energies in an effort to force the French King to submit to his claims of thoroughgoing papal supremacy. Three years later this politico-religious tug of war ended in the utter humiliation of the "Vicar of Christ," and immediately led to a catastrophic decline in the political and moral influence of the Church.

In 1305 a French bishop was elected Pope and took up official residence in Avignon, where he and his successors remained for more than seventy years. During this so-called period of the "Babylonian Captivity," the Popes steadily removed themselves and the Church organization from contact with the people and their parish priests. During the reign of John XXII, the greatest and most infamous of Avignonese Popes, a Spanish official trenchantly wrote:

> No poor man can approach the Pope. He will call and no one will answer because he has no money in his purse to pay.

The prestige of the Church was not enhanced by the re-entry of the Papacy to Rome in 1377. During the papal election of the following year the population of the Eternal City and the surrounding countryside forced the College of Cardinals to elect an Italian, (Urban VI), who would remain in Italy. However, the French cardinals refused to recognize Urban's election and, shortly after leaving Rome, elected a new Avignonese Pope, who became known as Clement VII. This began the Great Schism, which horrified pious Christians for the next forty years. (Interestingly enough, in the Bible the number "forty" connotes suffering.)

During these ignominious four decades two Popes attempted to carve up Christendom, each administering his "share" while anathematizing his counterpart. Meanwhile, the average Christian, who could look forward to little in life except a death, consecrated by the last rites, now was not even sure he could die in the odor of sanctity. No one knew whether a priest or bishop had been properly ordained and was therefore a bona fide dispenser of the sacraments. As a matter of fact, a popular rumor had it that no soul could pass through the gates of Heaven while Christianity was in schism. The end of the Great Schism in 1418 did little to arrest the alienation of large numbers of Christians from their Church. The story of the moral and spiritual degeneracy of certain Renaissance Popes need hardly be repeated here. Meanwhile, life was becoming more complex and difficult to cope with, as society passed from an agricultural into a commercial age. Obsolete knights were virtually obliged to live by robbery; while peasants and artisans, who had also been ruined by economic forces they neither understood nor could control, frequently rose in savage rebellion against their rural oppressors. This sorry state of affairs was further complicated and worsened by inevitable outbreaks of the plague.

By the early sixteenth century the aloofness, corruption, and taxation policies of the Papacy, which were further complicated by rampant simony and the indulgence traffic, made many Europeans ready at last for a Reformation. This was poignantly realized by Erasmus, who desperately tried to induce the Christian Church to put its house in order before disaster struck.

In particular he felt that the Church had lost sight of its proper function—the care of man's spirit and soul; and he had only contempt for its overconcern with empty ritualism and useless learning. Yet Erasmus' sardonic criticisms did not prompt him either to leave the Church or advocate the destruction of its organization. He felt religion was primarily a matter of the spirit and soul, and that the fundamental nature of man's relationship to God could not be appreciably altered by joining a new sect.

Like his scholarly colleague, Martin Luther wanted to reform the Church from within; and it required far more

than his vituperatively anti-papal comments to make
him into a heretic. Not until Luther's disputation with
John Eck did the former even question the divine ap-
pointment of the Papacy or work out the natural conclusions to his "priesthood of all believers" concept.
Moreover, the basic religious conservatism of the Wit-
tenberg friar quickly emerged once Lutheranism became
established. He was horrified at the spectre of social
revolution, loathed the Anabaptist sects, and presided
over his flock in as pontificating a manner as that of the
Pope who had excommunicated him.

As a matter of fact by the mid-twentieth century,
German Lutheranism has become so traditionalist that
its hymns are frequently sung in Catholic Churches!
Quite understandably then, shortly after it shaped up,
Lutheranism left much to be desired in the minds of
other religious reformers, who subsequently founded
new, sometimes more militant, movements. Consequently, the early sixteenth century witnessed the
apogee of religious and intellectual extremism.

Erasmus, who had prophesied that the initial break
from the Church Universal would simply lead to many
more with resulting bitterness, confrontation, and fanaticism, tried to convince all sides in the Reformation
struggle of the need for moderation and compromise.
He failed miserably, and for his troubles earned the dis-
trust of Catholics and the hatred of Protestants.

* * * * *

When the second generation of Protestants assumed
the leadership of the Reformation movements, it proved
to be more aggressive and systematic in nature, with less
tolerance for any religious deviations. Within his
Genevan theocracy, John Calvin scorned and persecuted
the compromising intellectual. Bolsec's challenge of the
principles of predestination earned this conscientious
physician an ignominious banishment. Servetus' reflec-

tions on the nature of the trinity and his religious eclecticism resulted in his execution, perpetrated in the most diabolical fashion.

Castellio protested against the ubiquitous intolerance that made Church leaders into "bloodthirsty killers out of zeal for Christ." In his important treatises he maintained consistently that religious toleration was at the very basis of Christian morality. But Castellio was generally ignored, as hatreds between the various Christian sects were not yet ready to subside, and the era of religious extremism gave no indication of passing.

* * * * *

As the century further progressed, divisions within the realm of Protestantism appeared with great frequency. Lutherans were mocked and denounced by Calvinists and followers of Zwingli, who in turn could hardly get along with each other. When Melanchthon nobly tried to bridge the gap between these and other Protestant persuasions, he became universally despised by the objects of his efforts.

Then came the inevitable political prostitution of religion, first taking form in the indecisive Schmalkaldic wars, which were temporarily checked by the equally indecisive Peace of Augsburg. The guiding principle of this agreement, which in reality amounted to little more than a truce, was *cujus regio ejus religio*, (he who reigns, his the religion.) The formula applied only to Catholics and Lutherans, leaving Calvinists without legal status in Germany. Moreover, if the ruler of a particular German state had espoused an unpopular faith, some religious thinkers felt he should either be demoted, assassinated, or forcibly ousted from any official position.

By mid century anyone who even considered negotiating compromise settlements between Catholics and Protestants did so at the risk of his life. It is little wonder that in some highly sophisticated intellectual circles an attitude of thoroughgoing religious skepticism set in. Charron's fideism bore a sad testimony to the deterioration of the sixteenth century religious scene.

* * * * *

Although most major European states were sooner or later afflicted by adverse political ramifications of the prevailing religious extremism, it was France that suffered the most. For three decades after the death of Henry II French soil was continually dampened with the blood of Catholics and Protestants, who served as cannon fodder for the armies of the "Holy League" and the Huguenot Party.

The last of the Valois kings were such pathetically ineffective rulers that without significant outside assistance they could never have managed to retain control of their realm, nor could they have prevented indigenous centrifugal forces from blowing it apart. Fortunately, the much-needed help was provided by their mother, the much-maligned Catherine de Medici.

Careful observance of the bitter legacy of Reform and Counter-Reform infused her with nothing but contempt for the ability of ecclesiastics and pious intellectuals to put their own houses in order. It seemed perfectly clear to the widow of Henry II that the only feasible solution to the multifarious domestic problems, created by rampant religious extremism, was a political one. The calls for moderation that had been made by Erasmus, Castellio, Melanchthon, and likeminded individuals were no doubt respected by Catherine, who recognized and endorsed their legitimacy. However, since she was, if nothing else, a hardheaded realist, the Queen-Mother knew that these pleas had as much chance of being heeded as did the proverbial voices crying in the wilderness. She therefore tirelessly combed her brain for techniques—Machiavellian and not-so-Machiavellian—to employ in her attempt to sap the energy from those inspired fanatics who were capable of destroying France.

In her repertoire of conciliatory measures and devices were countless amnesties for perennial troublemakers, a never-ending series of compromise peace settlements for the armies of the "Holy League" and the Huguenot Party, numerous edicts of toleration and attempts to establish freedom of conscience as a royal policy, the Colloquy of Poissy and its offshoots, significant cooperation with the *Politique* party, and of course the celebrated "Flying Squadron." Indeed, Catherine made only one mistake in her efforts to glue France together. Unfortunately it was a tragic one, the St. Bartholemew's Day Massacre.

In the end she failed. Yet her methods were for the most part the only ones that, under the circumstances, made any sense. As a matter of fact, many of them were destined to be imitated by her son-in-law, the future Henry IV, who by the turn of the century did indeed successfully manage to put an end to the French "time of troubles."

In his distinguished essays on Catherine de Medici, J.E. Neale accused the Queen-Mother of having been "completely lacking in the qualities of a statesman." One might well ask Sir John just what *he* would have done to lead France out of its agony, had he been regent during the reigns of Charles IX and Henry III!

* * * * *

In dealing with religious difficulties across the Channel, Elizabeth was in many ways more fortunate than the widow of Henry II. Unlike the latter she was a completely legitimate ruler, who consistently demonstrated to her subjects that she was "one of them" and would do nothing that would ever be injurious to the realm.

Moreover, she was a striking, highly dignified woman, endowed with a native brilliance that surpassed Catherine's above-average intelligence. Elizabeth constantly mingled and frolicked with her people, adding a human touch to her reign, which was virtually absent from that of her French counterparts. Quite fortunately for her, the English crown had no Condés, Colignys, or Guises with which to contend, and was less vulnerable, thanks to its splendid insularity, to the pious onslaught of enemy missionaries. Finally, the exceptionally talented advisors who guided, albeit not definitively, Elizabeth's every political move easily dwarfed in competence the well-meaning but ill-starred Michel de l'Hospital.

Yet the fact remains that the second daughter of Henry VIII was confronted with a major threat of civil strife fed by religious extremism. Elizabeth had to undo the damage caused by the three preceding reigns, knowing full well that success would come in this endeavor only if she completely eschewed the sledge hammer approach to the resolution of problems. Put differently, as was the case with Catherine de Medici, the Good Queen Bess was obliged to move subtly and opportunistically, freely using the author of the *Prince* as her guide. Moreover, she never lost sight of the fact that only a royal policy based in general on the politics of moderation, compromise, and conciliation could save England from the horror which France had to endure for thirty miserable years.

* * * * *

As has been previously noted, the tragedy of Catherine's response to the French religious crisis was that it was cursed by one major tactical mistake. Elizabeth committed *no* serious blunders. Interestingly enough however, the successors to these remarkable women varied significantly in their ability to deal with the religious situations that each inherited. Immediately upon his accession to the throne, James I clearly demonstrated his inability and unwillingness to espouse a *politique* position in order to help bridge the gap between the several sects with which he had to deal. In answer to Catholic pleas for toleration, the King of England replied with a statement of his intentions of rigidly enforcing all anti-Catholic legislation. Such ill-advised policies shortly provoked an attempt, engineered by English Jesuits, to blow up the entire establishment with gunpowder. It was a near miss.

With regard to the other end of the religious spectrum, James I was equally myopic, equating any deviation from his brand of Anglicanism with a threat to the crown. At the Hampton Court Conference of 1604, a delegation of Puritans presented him with a petition requesting toleration of their views, which were not totally imcompatible with Anglican latitudinarianism. Refusing to recognize the loyalty and moderation of these conscience-stricken subjects, the King reacted to their plea with brutal frankness, stating simply to them: "No bishop, no King."

In short, James I had at his disposal a multitude of historical lessons, which could have greatly assisted him in coping with the vicissitudes of his reign. In particular, his predecessor had bequeathed to him a virtual blueprint for the attainment of religious tranquility. He simply refused to follow it, with disasterous results for his realm and his son, the unfortunate Charles I.

* * * * *

On the other hand, not only did Henry Bourbon learn from the mistakes of his predecessors, he also presided over a type of religious settlement that would have had an excellent chance of succeeding in England as well as in France. A son-in-law of Catherine de Medici and closest surviving relative to the last Valois King, Henry was by the 1580's next in line for the French throne. The Bourbon's candidacy was further strengthened when, on his deathbed, Henry III ordered that his brother-in-law succeed him.

When the heir apparent to the throne experienced military opposition to his legitimate claims, he neutralized most of it with shattering efficiency. And as it became clear to him that the French capital, a Catholic stronghold, would not surrender to his armies, he simply abjured his Huguenot faith, allegedly muttering the words: "Paris is worth a Mass."

Once officially crowned at the famous Chartres Cathedral, the new king, taking the name Henry IV, disposed of remaining extremist Catholic opponents in the only sensible way—bribery. With the payment of sixty million *livres*, what was left of the "Holy League" retired in defeat, but very comfortably.

The Protestant problem was handled by the enactment of the Edict of Nantes in 1598. Among its many provisions this law granted Protestants freedom of worship on their own estates and in those towns where Protestantism had been the faith of most inhabitants before 1597. Non-Catholics were also protected against discrimination in schools, courts of law, and employments.

Although no Protestant worship would be tolerated in and around Paris or in any episcopal towns, all but extremist Huguenots recognized the magnanimity and workability of the Edict of Nantes. Moreover, in order to guarantee that all its promises would be fulfilled, the Protestants were allowed to maintain their control of about 100 fortified places; and the expenses incurred by this were to be absorbed by the Catholic King.

That the Edict of Nantes made good *political* sense was apparent when of all people, the Jesuits endorsed it, realizing as did Henry IV that the revolutionary piece of legislation constituted the only alternative to continued religious civil war. As a matter of fact, it could even be argued that in the long run, Henry's law actually sounded the death knell for French Protestantism; because in providing for its existence in only a fixed number of areas, the edict effectively precluded its expansion. In 1685 Henry's grandson would easily be able to all but destroy the remains of the Reformation in France.

* * * * *

* * * * *

By the beginning of the seventeenth century important societies and governments finally managed to stabilize themselves. The one institution most responsible for this new stability was the sovereign—paradoxically the very one which in the days of Luther helped create situations that led to religious civil war. Just as many princes in the early sixteenth century readily entered the controversial area of religion to augment their own power, most subsequently realized that the faith of Christians, like the plague, had such devastating potentialities that whatever gains they had made were in jeopardy by the final third of the century.

European rulers grew to realize that in order to safeguard the interests of their realm, religion somehow had to be disciplined and controlled. Yet the difficulties of arriving at this ideal situation could hardly be overstated, in view of the fact that those powerful sectarian organizations which had come into existence during decades of religious strife were intent upon maintaining their independence and struggling with their adversaries until a definitive victory had been won. It was only the exceptional and determined sovereign who could steer an even course in religious policy and successfully stop the various churches in his realm from fighting a war that they had begun and were incapable of terminating.

* * * * *

A Selected Bibliography

The following book list is intended to provide the introductory student with some additional works which he might consult to broaden his knowledge of the various topics dealt with in this study.

Armstrong, F., *The French Wars of Religion*, 2nd ed., Oxford, 1904.

Bainton, R.H., *Erasmus of Christendom*, New York, 1965.

——, *Here I Stand; A Life of Martin Luther*, New York, 1950.

——, *The Hunted Heretic. The Life and Death of Michael Servetus, 1511-1553*, Boston, 1953.

——, *The Travail of Religious Liberty. Nine Biographical Studies*, Philadelphia, 1951, pp. 72-94, 97-124.

Baird, H.M., *History of the Rise of the Huguenots*, 1880, 2 vols.

——, *The Huguenots and Henry of Navarre*, 1886, 2 vols.

Beard, C., *The Reformation of the Sixteenth Century in Relation to Modern Thought and Knowledge*, 1883.

Bohmer, H., *The Road to Reformation*, Philadelphia, 1946.

Bromily, G.W., *Zwingli and Bullinger*, Library of Christian Classics, 1953.

Carrière, Abbé B., *Les Épreuves des Églises de France au XVIième Siècle*, 1936.

Chambers, R.W., *Thomas More*, 1935.

Church, W.F., *Constitutional Thought in Sixteenth Century France*, Cambridge, Mass., 1941.

Darby, H.S., *Hugh Latimer*, 1953.

Dickens, A.G., *Thomas Cromwell and the English Reformation*, 1959.

Duby, G. and Mandrou, R., *Histoire de la Civilization Française*, 1958, 2 vols.

Elton, G.R., *England under the Tudors*, 1955.

Fagniez, G., *L'Economie Sociale de la France sous Henry IV, 1589-1610*, 1897.

Farner, O., *Huldrych Zwingli*, Zurich, 1943-60, 4 vols.

——, *Zwingli, the Reformer*, 1952.

Fife, R.H., *The Revolt of Martin Luther*, New York, 1957.

Green V.H.H., *Luther and the Reformation*, New York, 1964.

Haag, E. and E., *La France Protestante*, 1846-59, 10 vols.

Hughes, P., *The Reformation in England*, 1950, 53-54, 3 vols.

Huizinga J., *Erasmus and the Age of the Reformation*, New York, 1957.

Hunt, R.N.C., *John Calvin*, London, 1933.

Hyma A., *The Youth of Erasmus*, 2nd ed., New York, 1968.

Imbart de la Tour, P., *Les Origines de la Réforme*, Melun, 1946, 4 vols.

Kingdon, Robert M., *Geneva and the Coming of the Wars of Religion in France, 1555-1563*, Geneva, 1956.

Knappen, M.M., *Tudor Puritanism*, Chicago, 1939.

Knowles, D., *The Religious Orders in England*, Cambridge, 1959, vol. 3.

Kooiman, W.J., *By Faith Alone*, 1954.

Lamar, Jensen, D., *Diplomacy and Dogmatism. Bernardine de Mendoza and the French Catholic League*, Cambridge, Mass., 1963.

Lecler, J., *Toleration and the Reformation*, London, 1960, 2 vols.

Leonard, E.G., *Histoire Générale du Protestantisme*, 1961, 2 vols.

Lindsay, T.M., *History of the Reformation*, Edinburgh, 1906-7, 2 vols.

Mackinnon, J., *Luther and the Reformation*, London, 1925-1930, 4 vols.

Maulde-la-Clavière, M.A.R. de, *Les Origines de la Révolution Francaise au Commencement du XVIième Siècle*, Paris, 1889.

McNeil, J.T., *The History and Character of Calvinism*, New York, 1954.

Muller, J.A., *Stephen Gardiner and the Tudor Reaction*, 1926.

Neale, J.E., *The Age of Catherine de Medici*, 1960.

Nef, J.U., *Industry and Government in France and England, 1540-1640*, Philadelphia, 1940.

Olin, J.C., ed., *Luther, Erasmus, and the Reformation: A Catholic-Protestant Reappraisal*, New York, 1969.

Parker, T.M., *The English Reformation to 1588*, 1950.

Pelikan, J.J., *Spirit versus Structure. Luther and the Institutions of the Church*, New York, 1968.

Phillips, M.M., *Erasmus and the Northern Renaissance*, New York, 1965.

Pollard, A.F., *Henry VIII*, 1905.

——, *Thomas Cranmer and the English Reformation*, 1905.

——, *Wolsey*, 1929.

Powicke, F.M., *The Reformation in England*, 1941.

Romier, Lucien, *Catholiques et Huguenots à la cour de Charles IX*, 1924.

——, *La Conjuration d'Amboise*, Paris, 1923.

——, *Le Royaume de Catherine de Médicis*, 1922, 2 vols.

Rupp, E.G., *Studies in the Making of the English Protestant Tradition*, 1947.

Shweibert, E.G., *Luther and his Times*, St. Louis, 1950.

Smyth, C.H., *Cranmer and the Reformation under Edward VI*, Cambridge, 1926.

Thompson, J.W., *The Wars of Religion in France, 1559-1576*, Chicago, 1909.

Van Dyke, Paul, *Catherine de Medicis*, London, 1923, 2 vols.

Vienot, J., *Histoire de la Réforme Française des Origines à l'Édit de Nantes*, 1926, 2 vols.

Wendel, F., *Calvin; The Origin and Development of his Religious Thought*, London, 1963.

Whitehead, A.W., *Gaspard de Coligny, Admiral of France*, London, 1904.

Wilbur, E.M., *A History of Unitarianism*, vol. 1, Cambridge, Mass., 1947.

Wilkenson, Maurice, *A History of the League or Sainte Union*, Glasgow, 1929.

Zweig, S., *Erasmus of Rotterdam*, New York, 1934.

——, *The Right to Heresy: Castellio versus Calvin*, New York, 1936.